Medicine, Magic and Religion

'The restraint, power and fineness of Rivers' mind make it impossible to be patient with critics who feel uncomfortable in the presence of his greatness.'

Robert Graves

'Despite the distinction and variety of his scientific achievements, only those personally acquainted with him can fully appreciate the causes of that profound respect with which he was regarded. ... *Medicine, Magic and Religion* is a document of first-rate importance ... and it will thus remain as a worthy monument to its distinguished author.'

Times Literary Supplement

'Always, as we read, we feel we are in close contact with a mind that is really thinking.'

Nation

W. H. R.
Rivers

Medicine, Magic and Religion

The Fitzpatrick Lectures delivered before the
Royal College of Physicians of London
in 1915 and 1916

With a preface by G. Elliot Smith

 London and New York

First published 1924
by Kegan Paul, Trench and Trübner
as part of the International Library of Psychology

First published in Routledge Classics 2001
by Routledge
11 New Fetter Lane, London EC4P 4EE
29 West 35th Street, New York, NY 10001

Routledge is an imprint of the Taylor & Francis Group

© 1924 W. H. R. Rivers

Typeset in Joanna by RefineCatch Limited, Bungay, Suffolk
Printed and bound in Great Britain by
TJ International Ltd, Padstow, Cornwall

British Library Cataloguing in Publication Data
A catalogue record for this book is available from the British Library

Library of Congress Cataloging in Publication Data
A catalog record for this book has been applied for

ISBN 0–415–25403–5

PREFACE

This book represents perhaps the first attempt to interpret with real knowledge and sympathetic insight the thoughts and ideas that find expression in Primitive Medicine. It is therefore a contribution of unique value to the history of medicine. But it is more than that; it is a revelation of the human mind and of the fundamental principles underlying the social practices and religious beliefs of the less sophisticated members of the human family. Moreover, this book crystallizes a particular phase of the development of Dr. Rivers's ethnological opinion, which is of special interest to those of his fellow-anthropologists who are striving to interpret the workings of the human mind in primitive societies.

After delivering the four Fitzpatrick Lectures at the Royal College of Physicians of London (in 1915 and 1916)—and issuing them in *The Lancet* in the form in which they were actually given—Dr. Rivers definitely postponed their publication as a book, which is required by the terms of the FitzPatrick endowment, until he had collected enough material to write a comprehensive treatise on Primitive Medicine. During the last six years of his life he amassed a vast collection of bibliographical references to the subjects dealt with in this book, and also, by correspondence from fieldworkers in ethnology in various parts of the world, a great deal of important evidence. But, unfortunately, his death occurred before he had begun to weave all this new information into the texture of the story so graphically told in the FitzPatrick Lectures. The addition by another hand of this material would not only have seriously delayed the issue of these important lectures in a form readily accessible to ethnologists, but would also have spoiled the symmetry of a work which, for various reasons, it is desirable to present as its author left it.

In his great monograph, The History of Melanesian Society, Dr. Rivers has revealed the earlier stages of his repudiation of what, at the time (1914) when it was published, was the fashionable doctrine in ethnology. During the last eight years of his life, his views were gradually undergoing a subtle change in the direction of the fuller recognition of the part played by the diffusion of culture in the development of custom and belief. These lectures represent a phase in this development which is of special interest, for they were planned and in part written at a time when two new and potent influences were at work. The first two chapters of the book were written in the autumn of 1915, when Dr. Rivers had been working at the Maghull Military Hospital for three months investigating the mental effects of the stress and strain of trench-warfare. He was very keenly interested in the similarity of the methods practised in that hospital for diagnosing the psychical disabilities of soldiers and the processes he had been using in Melanesia to unravel the meaning of the social and religious practices of people of lowly culture. This impressive experience occurred in the summer of 1915, when Rivers's interest in ethnology was being deeply stirred by discussions of the

far-reaching effects of cultural diffusion in the history of civilization, and, by implication, of a new interpretation of the
psychological factors involved in the process. In this book the
effects of this dual stimulation find expression; and it is doubly
interesting because it represents a phase in the development of
views which became further modified after 1918 for reasons
indicated in his essay on "The Aims of Ethnology" in *Psychology
and Politics*. For this reason I have thought it useful to reprint (as
Chapter 5) a lecture on *Mind and Medicine*, delivered by him in
1919 at the John Rylands Library in Manchester. It deals with a
subject directly relevant to the rest of the book, but it also
reveals the trend of his thought at the time just before *Conflict
and Dream* was written.

Rivers never reached the stage of opinion represented in W. J.
Perry's *The Origin of Magic and Religion* (1923); but the latter work
gives expression to the general view towards which he was cau-
tiously moving. In 1915, when Rivers was preparing the first of
his FitzPatrick Lectures, he made the remark to me one day:
"Perry will make the broad generalizations and the big advance;
my function is to move forward step by step and to consolidate
the gains." This perhaps is an apt, if perhaps unduly modest,
appreciation of the task, one step of which he has achieved in
this book.

The fundamental aim of primitive religion was to safeguard
life, which was achieved by certain simple mechanical procedures based upon rational inference but often false premises.
Primitive medicine sought to achieve the same end, and not
unnaturally used the same means. Hence in the beginning
religion and medicine were parts of the same discipline, of
which magic was merely a special department. Dr. Rivers's suggestion (especially in Chapter 3) that the association of medicine with magic and religion may have been due to a blending of
different cultures is really an expression of the view that dominated his thoughts between 1911 and 1918, but from which he

was gradually becoming emancipated during the last four years of his life.

For their generous permission to reprint lectures fully reported in The Lancet and the Bulletin of the John Rylands Library, I must express my gratitude to the Editors of these journals.

G. ELLIOT SMITH

UNIVERSITY COLLEGE LONDON.
1st January, 1924.

NOTE TO SECOND EDITION

No alterations have been made in this Edition; but in Dr. Rivers's Psychology and Ethnology (1926) certain topics that are briefly mentioned in this book, such as massage (p. 91) and circumcision and incision (p. 95), are more fully discussed. The two books, in fact, are complementary the one to the other and should be read in conjunction by those who want to understand the development of Dr. Rivers's views in Ethnology and the present position of the study of mankind.

G. E. S.

November, 1926.

1

Medicine, magic, and religion are abstract-terms, each of which connotes a large group of social processes, processes by means of which mankind has come to regulate his behaviour towards the world around him. Among ourselves these three groups of process are more or less sharply marked off from one another. One has gone altogether into the background of our social life, while the other two form distinct social categories widely different from one another, and having few elements in common. If we survey mankind widely this distinction and separation do not exist. There are many peoples among whom the three sets of social process are so closely inter-related that the disentanglement of each from the rest is difficult or impossible; while there are yet other peoples among whom the social processes to which we give the name of Medicine can hardly be said to exist, so closely is man's attitude towards disease identical with that which he adopts towards other classes of natural phenomena.

METHODS OF INQUIRY

In any attempt to study a social institution there are three chief lines of approach and methods of inquiry. We may examine the institution historically, seeking to learn how it has been built up, how this advance has taken place here and that there; we may study the social conditions under which it has progressed in one place, been stationary in another, and degenerated in a third; and we may attempt to go back to its origin, and ascertain the steps by which it has become differentiated from other institutions, and has acquired an independent existence.

A second method is the psychological. We may attempt to study the states of mind, individual and collective, which underlie the acts, again individual and collective, the sum of which make up the institution in question.

The third method, which may be called the sociological method, is the inquiry into the relations of the social processes which we are attempting to study to other social processes, in order to determine the interactions between the two.

Since the object of the FitzPatrick Lectures is the study of the history of medicine, it might seem that the first of these three lines of inquiry should form their subject. This would certainly be so if medicine were everywhere the independent and self-contained institution which it is among ourselves; but if my opening statement is correct this is very far from being the case. A necessary preliminary to any knowledge of its history must be the study of its relations to those other social processes with which it is associated. This preliminary task will occupy us in these lectures, which will deal with certain prolegomena to the early history of medicine, rather than with the history of medicine itself.

It would be quite impossible within the scope of this book to deal with the subject exhaustively. My object will be rather to consider lines of inquiry by which the subject may be studied; and for this purpose I shall limit myself as far as possible to one part of the world, viz. Melanesia and New Guinea, which have been especially the field of my own researches, with occasional references to the allied culture of Australia. The time has gone by in sociology when we tried to understand human institutions by comparing examples taken at random from every part of the world. The present trend[1] in the science which deals with these matters is to limit inquiries to a series of related peoples. If we reach conclusions by means of such inquiries, we can then proceed to see if they will apply in other parts of the world.

DEFINITION OF THE SOCIAL PROCESSES

I must begin by defining the three kinds of social process which are to be the subject of our study. The distinction between magic and religion is one which has long tried the ingenuity of students of human society. Among many peoples, including those with whom this book will especially deal, it is far from easy to draw any definite line between the two, and we need a term which will include both. A word which is sometimes used in this sense in English is magico-religious, and, in default of a better, I shall use it occasionally in this book. The use of this word will imply a certain attitude towards the world. If the matter be looked at from our point of view, this attitude would be one in which phenomena are dealt with by supernatural means. I say if regarded from our point of view because, of course, the use of the word supernatural implies the existence of the concept of the natural, and it is just this concept, as we have it, which is lacking among the people with whom I shall deal. The essence of medicine, as we now understand it, is that it regards disease as a phenomenon subject to natural laws, to be treated as we treat any other department of nature. The distinction between the attitude of the modern practitioner of medicine and the magico-religious attitude depends on the difference

[1] [This was written in 1915. Since then there has been a change of attitude.]

in the concept of disease in the two cases. One chief object of this book will be to discover what is the nature of the concept of disease among those who fail to distinguish medicine from magic and religion.

While the main topic will thus be the nature of the concept of disease among certain peoples of rude culture, and the relation of this concept to those underlying magic and religion, it will be interesting to pay attention to the distinction between these two groups of social process. A full study of this distinction would take us too far from our main subject, and I must be content to use a provisional distinction, which will be useful for descriptive purposes. When I speak of magic, I shall mean a group of processes in which man uses rites which depend for their efficacy on his own power, or on powers believed to be inherent in, or the attributes of, certain objects and processes which are used in these rites. Religion, on the other hand, will comprise a group of processes, the efficacy of which depends on the will of some higher power, some power whose intervention is sought by rites of supplication and propitiation. Religion differs from magic in that it involves the belief in some power in the universe greater than that of man himself.

Magic and religion are thus differentiated from one another by their attitude towards the means by which man seeks to influence the universe around him. Medicine, on the other hand, is a term for a set of social practices by which man seeks to direct and control a specific group of natural phenomena—viz. those especially affecting man himself, which so influence his behaviour as to unfit him for the normal accomplishment of his physical and social functions—phenomena which lower his vitality and tend towards death. By a process of generalization, society has come to classify these phenomena together, and has distinguished them from other groups of natural phenomena under the name of disease. As I have already said, one of the chief tasks of this book will be to ascertain how far this notion of disease, this category of the morbid, exists among the peoples included in our field of study; and we shall do this mainly by means of an inquiry into the processes by which man reacts to those phenomena we call morbid.

CONCEPT OF DISEASE BY VARIOUS PEOPLES

One way of approaching the problem will be to inquire how far different groups of mankind have set apart certain members of the community to deal with the morbid. When we have evidence of such division and specialization of social functions, we shall have at the same time definite evidence that those who have reached this specialization of function have also reached a stage of thought in which they separate morbid from other natural phenomena. One point of nomenclature may be considered here. In dealing with the subject of medicine from the comparative point of view, and among peoples of rude culture, we are met by a difficulty arising out of the wealth of the English language in terms for practitioners of the healing art. When in this book I am to speak of those members of the community whose special business it is to deal with disease, am I to call them doctors, medical-men, medicine men, physicians, or what? Medicine-men might seem the most appropriate of these, in that it is not a term used of our own practitioners, and will thus carry with it no connotation derived from our civilization. It suffers, however, from the disadvantage that it comes to be widely used in anthropological literature for sorcerers and dealers in various forms of magic, who may have no dealing with the morbid, and certainly exercise no therapeutical activities. I propose therefore, to use the old English term "leech". When I speak of a leech I shall mean a member of society whose special function it is to deal with the cure of disease. He may have other functions, such as the formation of rain, the promotion of vegetation, or even the production of disease itself; but in so far as he is dealing with the cure of disease be will he, in the nomenclature I shall use, a leech.

One of the methods, then, by which we may seek to ascertain how far different peoples of the world distinguish morbid from other natural phenomena is by inquiring how far they distinguish the leech from the sorcerer or the priest. The chief line of inquiry, however, will be an examination of the processes by which man at different stages of culture deals with disease. We shall find that, even when there is no clear differentiation of the leech from other members of society, mankind has theories of the causation of disease, carries out proceedings which correspond with those we call diagnosis and prognosis, and finally has modes of treatment which, even if they have little in common with our own remedies, nevertheless may be regarded as making up a definite system of therapeutics.

I have said that one of my chief objects will be an attempt to discover the nature of the concept of disease held by different peoples. I must first say a word about what we mean when we speak of a people possessing and acting on such a concept. I do not mean such a clear concept as is held, say, by the writer of an European textbook of medicine, a concept capable of being expressed by the formula we call a definition. Such a concept is the result of a very advanced process of generalization and abstraction, and we all know how difficult it is to frame such a definition, even with the large system of exact knowledge which we possess. It is evident that when we speak of the concept of disease held by such a people as the Melanesians we mean no exactly formulated definition, but a more or less vague system of ideas, which, though not distinctly formulated by a people, yet directs their behaviour—their reactions towards those features of the environment which we have classified together under the category of disease.

BELIEFS AS TO CAUSATION OF DISEASE

One element of the concept of disease, and perhaps the most important, is that it includes within its scope the factor of causation. There are usually clear-cut ideas concerning the immediate conditions which lead to the appearance of disease. One happy result of this fact is that we are able to approach our subject by way of etiology, and are thus led to deal with the medicine of savage peoples from the same standpoint as that of modern medicine, which rests, or should rest, entirely upon the foundation of etiology. By starting from etiology we shall find ourselves led on as naturally to diagnosis and treatment, as is the case in our own system of medicine.

If we examine the beliefs of mankind in general concerning the causation of disease, we find that the causes may be grouped in three chief classes: (1) human agency, in which it is believed that disease is directly due to action on the part of some human being; (2) the action of some spiritual or supernatural being or, more exactly, the action of some agent who is not human, but is yet more or less definitely personified; and (3) what we ordinarily call natural causes.

Among ourselves there are indications of the presence of all three kinds of belief, and this was certainly so in the not very remote past. We now only think of human agency in cases of poison and injury, and then only as the means by which the action of natural causes has been directed. The second category still exists in the "hand of God" of our statutes, and in the oral rites of our religion, but has ceased to take any part in orthodox medicine, though it still plays some part in the behaviour of the laity towards disease. In the professional art of medicine, and in the practice of the majority of the laity, the attitude towards disease is directed by the belief in its production by natural causes, meaning by this a body of beliefs according to which disease comes into being as the inevitable result of changes in our environment quite independent of human or superhuman agency.

If, on the other hand, we examine the culture of any savage or barbarous people, we find that their beliefs concerning the causation of disease fall in the main into one or other or both of the first two categories, while in many cases the third category can hardly be said to exist, and even then we cannot assign the beliefs to the category of natural causation. I shall deal with these cases more fully in the second chapter. For the present I shall confine my attention to those cases in which the native ideas concerning causation bring them within the realm of magic or religion. In this chapter I shall deal with cases which must either be definitely classed with magic, or belong more nearly to this category than to that of religion.

It would greatly simplify the treatment of our subject if the line of cleavage between the cases of causation of disease by human and non-human agency corresponded with the distinction between magic and religion. When writing this book I was at one time inclined to throw the distinction between magic and religion on one side, and describe the facts with which I shall have to deal under the headings of human and non-human agency. Such a plan, however, would only have avoided a difficulty which it is better to face, for if we treat medicine from the sociological standpoint we must study it in relation to other recognized social processes. Unless we are prepared to throw the categories of magic and religion aside altogether, they cannot be ignored in any discussion of the social relations of medicine.

DISEASE OR INJURY ASCRIBED TO MAGIC

The concept of magic which at present holds good in sociology and ethnology is largely influenced by the art called by this name in our own Middle Ages. The best known form of mediaeval magic was one in which non-human, spiritual agents took a

most important part. These beings acted as the immediate pro-
ducers of disease and other effects, the magical character of the
proceedings resting on the belief that the non-human agents had
come in one way or another under the power of the human
magician.

The magic of many peoples of rude culture, including those
of the area with which I especially deal, differs widely from this
in that disease or injury is, in many cases, ascribed to purely
human agency, even when to us the real cause of the condition
would seem to be obvious. This mode of causation is not merely
brought into play to explain cases of illness which have no obvious antecedent, but also those in which what we should call the
natural cause is obvious. Thus, if a man is killed or injured by
falling from a tree in the Island of Ambrim in the New Hebrides,
the fall is not ascribed to a loose branch, or to some failure of co-
ordination of the movements of the climber, but the accident, as
we loosely call it, is put to the account of the sorcerer. It is
probable that the sequence of ideas in the Melanesian mind is
that, in a business so familiar as that of climbing trees, accidents
would not happen unless someone has interfered with the normal course of events. If a sorcerer had not loosened a branch, or
produced an illusion whereby the victim had seen a branch
where there was none, he would not have fallen to the ground.

Similarly, death or injury in battle is not ascribed to the
superior skill of the enemy, or to a failure of defence, but it is
believed that a sorcerer has directed the missile of the assailant,
or has interfered with the defensive motions of the victim, or the
integrity of his weapons. A case of snake-bite is not ascribed to
the act which, according to our ideas, is natural to a venomous
animal, but it is believed that the snake has been put in the path
of the victim by a sorcerer, or has been endowed with special
powers by a sorcerer; or it may even be held that the animal
which has bitten the victim is no ordinary snake, but the
sorcerer himself in snake-like form.

To those whose main category of the causation of disease is human agency there is a firmly rooted belief in this mode of production, not only where causation would otherwise be mysterious or unknown, but also in those cases where the cause would seem, even to the most uninstructed lay mind in our own community, to lie within the province we call natural. It may be noted, moreover, that such ideas concerning the causation of disease are not empty beliefs devoid of practical consequences, but act as the motives for processes of treatment in case of injury, or for acts of revenge if the magical process should lead to the death of the victim. If we were so to define magic as to identify it with the exclusive action of human beings, this part of our subject would soon be treated. The art of diagnosis would consist in the discovery of the human agent, and the essential elements in the treatment would be the use of measures which would lead the sorcerer to put an end to the actions by which he is effecting his maleficent purpose.

In addition to these cases of purely human agency, there are many others in which our records tell us explicitly of conditions closely similar to those of our own Middle Ages, in which the immediate cause of the disease is the action of some non-human being, who is either under the control of human agency from the beginning, or is capable of being brought under such control when it is desired to influence the results produced by its action. In such cases the methods of diagnosis and treatment are often indistinguishable from those employed where the morbid condition is ascribed to direct human agency. Disease or injury believed to be produced by spiritual agency is treated without any element of those processes of supplication and propitiation as would be necessary to bring them within the scope of our definition of religion.

In those cases in which a leech acts through the intermediation of non-human beings, our records often leave us in doubt whether the curative actions should be regarded as magical or religious. A decision on this question can only be reached through an exact knowledge of the rites, manual and verbal, by which the leech effects his purpose; and it is only rarely that fieldworkers record these, being too often content to base their opinions on inferences contaminated by ideas derived from their own sphere of knowledge and interest.

My own opinion—it is nothing but an opinion—is that, as our exact knowledge of the leechcraft of different parts of the world increases, we shall find that the religious element in medical rites has been underestimated, or even ignored where it exists. At any moment, however, in the history of a science we must base our arguments upon the recorded facts: and in the account which I shall give, my object will be to illustrate the difficulties and uncertainties of the subject, rather than lay down any definite conclusions.

The cases I shall consider in this chapter are those in which it is believed that disease is directly due to human agency, and those in which on the available evidence it would seem that the methods of diagnosis and treatment depend on power believed to be inherent in the leech and his rites, or become effective through the intermediation of non-human beings, who need no definite rites of propitiation and supplication to persuade them to intervene in the curative process. In considering these cases it will be useful to distinguish certain classes, according to the nature of the process by which it is believed that disease can be produced; the method of treatment being as a rule such as would follow from the nature of the cause.

Three main classes may be distinguished: (1) Those in which some morbific object or substance is projected into the body of the victim; (2) those in which something is abstracted from the body; and (3) those in which the sorcerer acts on some part of the body of a person or on some object which has been connected with the body of a person, in the belief that thereby he can act on the person as a whole. These three classes will now be considered in detail.

DISEASE ASCRIBED TO OBJECT OR INFLUENCE PROJECTED INTO VICTIM'S BODY

The class of cases in which the cause of disease is supposed to be some object or substance which has been projected into the body of the victim fall into two groups, according as the morbific objects have found their way into the body of the victim by direct human agency, or by the action of some non-human agent. Both kinds are of frequent occurrence in Australia, where material objects such as stones, crystals, fragments of bone, or leaves are believed to be projected into the body, in some cases by sorcerers, and in other cases by spiritual beings, who thus punish intrusion into their sacred haunts or other offence. Disease is also produced in this manner among the Massim of New Guinea.[1]

In Melanesia this mode of production of disease by the projection of material objects into the body seems to be exceptional. Where disease is believed to be due to such projection, it is usually held that some invisible influence has been projected into the body, and even where some material substance has been introduced, it is not supposed that the object itself produces the disease. This is ascribed rather to some morbific essence or effluvium, of which the material object is but the carrier and visible sign.

A good example of such a mode of production of disease, which occurs in more than one part of Melanesia, is by means of an instrument called, in the Banks Islands, *tamatetikwa*, or ghost-shooter. A mixture of leaves, a dead man's bones, and other ingredients are placed in a slender bamboo, which the sorcerer

---

[1] C. G. Seligmann, *The Melanesians of British New Guinea*, Cambridge, 1910.

holds in his hands, with the thumb over the open end, till he sees his enemy, when the removal of the thumb allows the evil influence to reach the victim. Dr. R. H. Codrington has recorded[1] some dramatic cases, in which this method was employed, that very well illustrate the profound belief in its efficacy. By means of suggestion the ghost-shooter will kill a powerful and healthy man in a couple of days. A less direct procedure, customary in the Banks Islands, and there called *talamatai*, is to wrap a parcel consisting of a dead man's bone, or part of an arrow which has killed a man, in leaves and place it on the path over which the person whom it is desired to injure will shortly pass. The magical principle will spring out of the bundle, and pass into the body of the victim.

In cases of illness thus caused by the introduction of morbific objects or essences into the body of the patient, the treatment follows directly from the etiology, its aim being to extract the object or essence from the body, and thus remove the cause of the disease. For this purpose it is not always, or even usually, necessary to discover the agent by whom the objects have been introduced. In communities that ascribe disease to this cause there are men and women who are believed to have the power of removing objects, usually by sucking some part of the body; after which a stone, crystal, or other object is shown to the patient, as having been removed by the process. Since, in many such cases, the disease has been produced by a suggestion, set in action by the knowledge of some cause of offence to one believed to have the power of producing disease in this way, the sight of the object thus said to have been removed effects a rapid cure in removing the suggestion. In some cases, and especially in those in which the projected substance is of an immaterial kind, it may be necessary to discover the agent who alone can remove what has been implanted in the body, and in this case some

---

[1] *The Melanesians*, London, 1891, p. 205.

method of divination is usually employed to discover by whom the disease has been produced.

DISEASE ATTRIBUTED TO ABSTRACTION OF PART OF BODY OR SOUL

The second mode of production of disease is that in which it is believed that something is abstracted from the body. Examples of this occur in Australia, where the abstraction of the kidney fat, or, perhaps more correctly, of the fat of the omentum, forms one of the most widely held beliefs. In New Guinea and Melanesia this belief does not, so far as we know, exist; but in many parts of these regions the people believe in the causation of disease by the abstraction of the soul or of some part of it. The Melanesian examples of this process, are all, so far as we know, due to spiritual agency.

Thus, in the Banks Islands, the *atai* or soul may be taken from a man by one of the spirits called *vui*. The treatment consists in the recovery of the soul by one called *gismana* whose *atai* leaves his body in sleep and seeks out the soul of the patient.[1]

Another example, of which we have a full record,[2] comes from the Gazelle Peninsula of New Britain and Duke of York Island, where it is believed that disease is produced by one of a group of beings called *kaia*, which have the body or tail of a snake and the head of a man. The *kaia* usually acts in this way on one who has intruded on its haunts, or taken fruit without proper authorization from trees in the district it inhabits.

If anyone falls ill in these places, the people resort to a process of divination to determine whether the disease is due to the action of a *kaia*, or has arisen in some other way. The diviner places under his arm-pit a piece of shell-money enclosed in a

[1] W. H. R. Rivers, *History of Melanesian Society*, Cambridge, 1914, vol. i, p. 165.
[2] J. Meier, *Anthropos*, vol. iii, 1908, p. 1005.

lime-strewn banana leaf, and falls into a sleep. He then learns, not only how the disease has been produced, but, if it is due to a *kaia*, he is able to tell the nature of the fault which has incurred the anger of the half-snake half-human being. The diviner, who also acts as a leech, then proceeds to carry out his treatment.

In the Duke of York Island, lying between the northern end of New Britain and the southern end of New Ireland, this treatment is as follows: The leech sprinkles lime on a dracaena leaf, enfolds it in a leaf of another kind, and places the packet so formed on a fire until it is almost carbonized. The patient then stands with raised arms, and the leech passes the hot packet over his body with movements resembling the curves of the body of a snake, while the patient stamps on the ground so as to shake off the influence of the *kaia*. Then the leech opens the packet and takes therefrom a pinch of the lime, over which he incants the following formula:—

"Lime of exorcism. I banish the octopus; I banish the *teo* snake; I banish the spirit of the *Ingiet* (a secret society); I banish the crab; I banish the water-snake; I banish the *balivo* snake; I banish the python; I banish the *kaia* dog (a special kind of dog, unlike the existing dog of New Britain, which forms one of the companions or familiars of the *kaia*. The other animals mentioned in the formula are also familiars of the *kaia*).

"Lime of exorcism. I banish the slimy fluid; I banish the *kete* creeping-plant; I banish To Pilana; I banish To Wuwu-Tawur; I banish Tumbal. One has sunk them right down deep in the sea. Vapour shall arise to hold them afar; clouds shall arise to hold them afar; night shall reign to hold them afar; darkness shall reign to hold them afar; they shall betake themselves to the depths of the sea."

This is a literal translation of the original. Father Meier gives the following as the expression of its full meaning:—

"This is lime for exorcism with which I drive away the octopus, the different kinds of snake, the spirit of the *Ingiet* and the *kaia* dog. This is the lime with which I drive away the slime of the *kaia* pool, the creeping-plant called *kete*, and the *kaia* called To Pilana, To Wuwu-Tawur, and Tumbal. I have sunk them and they are now below in the deepest depths of the sea. Thick vapour, impenetrable cloud, dark night and black darkness shall surround them and block their way for ever to the upper world so that they shall remain for ever in the infinite abyss of the sea."

When the formula is finished the leech blows the lime over the patient and more lime is smeared on his body, especially in the epigastric region, on the arms near the shoulders, and on the ears and great toes. The packet is then thrown away, and the upper part of a coconut three-quarters ripe is husked with the teeth, and a hole bored in the shell round which red ochre is smeared. The leech then rubs in his hands the bloom of a species of mint, puts the fragments in the nut, and utters the following formula over the nut to act upon its milk:—

"The coconut of exorcism. I banish the slime of the *kaia*; I banish the slime of the crab; I banish every pool with yellow slime; away with every swarm of *teo* snakes; away with the spittle of the *teo* snake; away with To Wuwu-Tawur; away with all the sap of the *kete* creeper; away with every *alai-pukai* creeper; away with all red-brown water (water containing reddish algae).

"I banish every water of the *kaia*; away with every octopus; away with all the blood of the tree-snake.

"I banish every puffed-up belly; I banish every dried-up shrub and grass; I will fetch his soul again from the hollow of the *kaia*." (The *kaia* are said to dwell in hollows in the hills.)

The leech then bespatters the patient with saliva, gives him the coconut to drink, takes his fee, and goes.

This production of disease by the *kaia* comes in several respects very near the domain of religion, but I have included an account of the proceedings connected with it in this chapter because the treatment bears no evidence whatever of any appeal to, or propitiation of, higher powers. The attitude towards the *kaia* itself is evidently that of the exorcist acting on a being who is believed to be capable of control by the leech through his knowledge of the proper rites, manual and verbal. It is, of course, possible that behind the whole proceedings there may be the idea of appeal to some higher power of which the formulas provide no evidence; but we can only act on the evidence before us, and this shows no trace of any such idea. We have here an example of social activity which we must provisionally label as magic, but of a magic which differs fundamentally from that of the Australian or inhabitant of Torres Straits, a magic which approaches in its general character, as well as in many of its details, that of our own Middle Ages. It is not a process by which one person counteracts the injurious influence of another person, but one by which a human being, through the knowledge of the appropriate rites, is able to act upon a non-human being in such a way as to counteract his influence.

MAGICAL ACTION ON SEPARATED PART OF VICTIM'S BODY OR TOUCHED OBJECT

The third kind of process which I have included under the heading of magic is that in which disease is believed to be produced by acting upon some separated part of the body of the victim, or on some object which has been in contact with him. This kind of magic, usually known as sympathetic magic, has been so frequently considered[1] that it is hardly necessary to consider cases in detail. I propose to confine my attention to one example, which may help us to understand the exact nature of the process more clearly than has hitherto been possible. This example has only recently been recorded by Keysser,[2] a missionary among the

---

[1] See especially J. G. Frazer, *The Magic Art*, London, 1911. For examples from Melanesia, cf. Rivers, *op. cit.*, i, 156.

[2] In *Deutsch Neu-Guinea*, by R. Neuhauss, Berlin, 1911, vol. iii, p. 135.

Kai, an inland people of the north-eastern part of New Guinea. This procedure is of especial interest in that it shows the presence among this people of ideas concerning sympathetic magic which brings it into close relation with our second category, in which disease is produced by the abstraction of something from the body. According to Keysser, the Kai believe in a soul-substance which permeates not only every part of the body, but also extends its presence to anything which has been in contact with the body. When a sorcerer secures part of the body of his proposed victim, or an object which has been in contact with his body, he is believed to be really securing part of the soul of the person, and it is by the action of his magical processes upon this isolated portion of the soul that the rites of the sorcerer produce their effect.

A sorcerer who thus secures part of the soul-substance of one whom he wishes to injure, repairs to a lonely hut situated in a spot reputed to be the haunt of a ghost or other spiritual being, so that it is avoided by all except those who have undergone special initiation into this mode of magic, or have in some other way acquired knowledge which enables them to visit the spot with impunity. Often several sorcerers act in concert, each performing the rites I am about to describe, at first independently and later in concert.

The fragment of the body of the victim, or of something which he has touched, by means of which the sorcerer acts, is called *gâ*. It may be hair, a drop of sweat, excrement, remains of food, or even a piece of weed which the victim has touched. The *gâ* must have been freshly removed from, or been in contact with, the body of the victim, so that the sorcerer can be confident that it still contains the soul-substance of his victim. In order to ensure its retention the *gâ* is put at once in a piece of bamboo, which is hidden and kept warm by being placed in the arm-pit of the sorcerer. The *gâ* must not be taken near fire or smoke, nor must it be brought into contact with water, or with any sharply pointed object, for all these conditions tend to expel the soul-substance from its resting-place.

As soon as possible the sorcerer wraps the *gâ* in a leaf of which caterpillars are fond, with the idea that, as the leaf is eaten by caterpillars, so will the body of the victim be eaten by worms. The *gâ* wrapped in the leaf is put in a small bamboo, which must have been taken from a place inhabited by ghosts or spirits. Fragments of the bark of certain trees are added to the packet; some are added in order to make it heavy, for it is by means of the weight of the packet that one judges whether the soul-substance is present or has disappeared. Another tree, the bark of which is added, has a very thick stem, and is used in the hope that the body of the victim will swell, while the bark of the other trees is added on account of their evil smell. The bamboo and bark are wrapped in another leaf and bound up with a creeper which withers very quickly, pointing thus to the rapid wasting and death of the victim. The packet so made is closely bound till it is just of a size to go into a larger piece of bamboo, which must also come from the abode of a ghost or spirit. This is put in yet another bamboo, which is sealed with the inspissated sap of a tree and covered with shells. As the packet is thus wrapped and sealed, the sorcerer calls to the white cockatoo: "Cockatoo, Cockatoo, come and tear open the body of X; bite his entrails to pieces so that he dies." The packet is then bound to a rod, and over it are sung words by means of which the spirits are summoned from the hollow where they dwell to take the soul of the victim to the home of the dead. The packet is wrapped in a prickly creeper so that the body of the victim shall be tormented with painful stings, and then in a leaf with fine hairs which tickle and irritate the skin, and the whole is wrapped in a withered leaf of the bread-fruit tree, with the idea that, as the leaf falls to the ground, so shall the body of the victim wither and fall into the grave.

During all these proceedings the sorcerer murmurs: "Oha and

Wakang; ye two giant lizards; lay yourselves on his soul and press upon it so that all joyful springing and all pleasure shall cease. Stop his ears so that he no more hears and his thoughts become confused." As these words are uttered the sorcerer beats with his open hand upon the packet, in order that painful blows may affect the body of the victim. The packet is then bound once more with a creeper, while the following formula is uttered: "Fall and rot like the gherkins. Let the victim disappear in pains. May his limbs writhe in pain. May his whole body writhe in pain. May his entrails become contracted in pain. May his generative organs be distorted in pain." These proceedings are not carried out once merely, but are repeated again and again, it may be for many months.

Every other day the sorcerer enters the lonely hut where he keeps the imprisoned soul and treats it in this way, putting the packet on each occasion upon the ashes of the fire, and this goes on until the victim begins to sicken, when the proceedings enter upon a new phase. The packet is heated at the fire after being covered with fine prickles, and the bark of a tree covered with tubercles is added so that the body of the victim may be covered with similar lumps. The packet is bespattered with the chewed root of a hot peppery plant so that the victim shall have fever. The fire at which the packet is heated must be made only of certain woods and of a creeper, the section of which darkens when it is cut, with the idea that the skin of the victim shall darken and his blood become black. Every day, if possible, the packet is laid on the fire with the words:

> "Eagle and Hawk. Ye both, here is your prey. Seize it with sharp claws.
> Rend his body and tear it to pieces. Then may corruption and worms, maggots and beetles utterly destroy his body."

At every repetition of this spell the packet is turned round by an assistant, while the sorcerer himself mimics the agony of his victim. He cries, shouts, and groans, as if in pain. He complains to his friends who visit him, and prays for help and sympathy, and his assistant comforts him in the way of one who visits a friend in so grievous a situation. Finally, the sorcerer groans like a dying man, imitates the death-rattle, draws his last breath, and pretends to be dead. Before leaving the packet for similar treatment on another day he puts it between pieces of wood weighed down with a stone, and covers the whole with ashes.

In order to reassure himself from time to time that the soul is still in the packet, the sorcerer goes to the hut in the darkness and listens. If he hears a rustling in the roof of the hut, or any other sound, he is satisfied that the soul is still there, and that his labours still await their reward. To assist his purpose, however, he must submit to many hardships and restrictions. He must not bathe nor let rain touch his skin. He may only drink the water of puddles which have been heated in the sun, for the cool water of a stream would allay the burning fever of his victim. Even pure water of any kind may be regarded as unsafe, and the sorcerer may drink only water which has been used for cooking. He must not eat boiled vegetables, but must roast his taro at a fire. During the whole proceedings he must abstain from sexual intercourse, nor should he take food from men who have not so abstained.

In the hut where the packet is kept there must be deathly silence. No one must speak aloud nor cough loudly. All conversation must be conducted in whispers. No wood may be broken, and such noise as that produced by treading on twigs must be avoided. The hut itself consists of two chambers, in the smaller of which the packet is kept, and no light is allowed to enter this chamber, so that the imprisoned soul may receive no ray of hope for its escape.

The whole proceedings reach their climax at a feast which has brought together the people of many parts. The sorcerer and his companions leave the rest, and assemble in the lonely hut. All those who have been carrying out these rites bring their bundles with them. These are weighed on the open hand, so as to judge whether the soul is still present, and those found to be too light are set aside. The rest are put in an old pot covered with sherds, strewn with ashes, and surrounded with a ring of fire. Then the sorcerers imitate the sickness of the victim, after which the packets are taken from the spot and laid on an open fire so that the outer coverings are consumed, with the idea of bringing the disease of the victim to a crisis. The sorcerers writhe as if in mortal pain, sigh, groan, and utter loud complaints. Their friends visit them, pity them, and express opinions about the people by whom they may have been bewitched. While some of the sorcerers are thus simulating mortal sickness, others take the packets from the fire and wring them between pieces of cloth, with the idea that the victim shall be smitten with mortal agony, his throat and heart pressed together, his breath driven out, and he himself driven to death by terror and despair. The pieces of cloth are cut and each packet falls to the ground, while some mimic the death of the victim and others utter his death-wail. At the same time a tree in the neighbourhood is felled, to which the name of the victim is given.

Finally the packet is thrown in the fire so that the coverings are completely burnt, and the bamboo vessels within it are wrapped in bark and beaten violently with a stone, while the death-scene is again portrayed. While some lie as if dead upon the ground, others talk about them and their affairs and put on women's head-dresses and wail as if they were women. They utter the reproaches of one village against another, and threaten fearful revenge. The wordy war leads to blows, and with cudgels and sticks to represent weapons the sorcerers fight in mockery of the combat which will follow the death of the victim.

TREATMENT: MAGICAL OR RELIGIOUS
NATURE OF RITES

The treatment of the morbid conditions produced by these magical proceedings is inspired by beliefs of the same order, consisting of measures to counteract the rites of the sorcerer. The method frequently found elsewhere, in which the sorcerer himself is induced by payments or other means to remove his spell, in this case to release the imprisoned soul-substance, is not mentioned by Keysser, but the release of the soul is brought about by other means. A friend of the victim may secretly free the soul from its prison, or the liberation may be effected in a symbolic manner. A magical receptacle, in which some soul-substance has been put, is rubbed against the breast, back, and legs of the patient, to portray the return of his own soul-substance to his body; and the receptacle is then torn asunder to show that the soul is free. The action is repeated three times, on each occasion with a different formula, and by the power of these actions the soul-substance which has not been sufficiently closely bound can again be made free. The principle underlying another method is that of the extinction of fire by water, some of the soul-substance of the patient being placed in the cool water of a mountain stream. In still another method some of the soul-substance of the patient is enclosed in leaves and hidden within a hollow stone, which is then thrown into a deep pool. The therapeutical measures thus employed by the Kai in order to cure disease produced by magic thus reveal the same dependence of treatment on etiology which we have found among other peoples and in proceedings of other kinds.

These elaborate rites of the Kai would be regarded by all ethnologists as an example of magic, but they have several features which bring them very near to religion. The formulas are not decisive in this respect, though more than one seems to have in it a note of appeal to higher powers. Still more significant of the religious attitude is the ordinance that certain of the objects used in the rites must have come from the abode of ghosts or spirits. The methods of treatment, on the other hand, seem to be purely magical, and taking the rites as a whole they must certainly be regarded as magical rather than religious.

CONCRETE NATURE OF BELIEFS UNDERLYING THE RITES

The rites of the Kai provide characteristic examples of the two kinds of sympathetic magic, known respectively as imitative, or homœopathic, and contagious magic. The principle which has hitherto been held to underlie these forms of magic is of a more or less mysterious kind.

Thus, Sir James Frazer[1] refers the belief in the connexion between a person and a separated part of his body to a relation "which we may conceive as a kind of invisible ether, not unlike that postulated by modern science for a precisely similar purpose—namely, to explain how things can physically affect one another through a space which appears to be empty".

Sir James Frazer does not, of course, intend this explanation of contagious magic to be anything more than a figurative expression, in the language of modern science, of the modes of thought which determine the actions of savage man. Into whatever equivalents, however, we translate his language, the ideas thus held to form the basis of contagious magic will have an abstract, if not mystical, character which I believe to be opposed to the concrete nature of the mental processes of peoples of rude culture. Often the savage performs rites of the most complex kind merely because this course of action has been prescribed for him by the immemorial traditions of his community, but where direct motives for his actions can be discovered they have

[1] *Op. cit.*, vol. i, p. 54.

a concrete character very different from that suggested by the metaphor of Sir James Frazer.

The special interest of the blend of medicine and magic practised by the Kai lies in the concrete and definite character of the beliefs which underlie these elaborate rites. The savage has few concepts more definite than that of the soul and of its continued existence after death. We have only to qualify this concept by the addition of the belief that the soul is divisible to give us the principle which underlies the magic of the Kai, a principle as definite as any of those which underlie the religious conduct of civilized man. The contagious magic of the Kai rests, not on any mystical belief in action at a distance, but on the belief that the sorcerer has in his possession part of the soul of another person, part of the vital essence of the person which he wishes to destroy. The conduct of the sorcerer might be held to imply a belief that action upon the part is equivalent to action upon the whole, but it is probable that there is rather confusion between part and whole, or more correctly, in the case of the Kai, between soul and soul-substance. That this is so is suggested by the confusion between soul and soul-substance which occurs in several parts of the account given by Keysser.

We only know of the concept of a divisible soul-substance in New Guinea and the Malay Archipelago, and we must await further evidence to show how widely diffused it is throughout the world. All that we can say now is that this concept affords an explanation of much in the ways of savage man which is at present mysterious and unintelligible.

There is probably little justification for ascribing the other main variety of sympathetic magic to any vague mysterious principle. The rites of the Kai are full of acts which show a belief in the efficacy of imitation, many of their features depending on the idea that the imitation of an event will bring that event to pass. This principle, often summed up in the phrase, "like produces like," is one in which there is nothing vague or indefinite.

It may only seem so to the more scientific of our number because we have ceased to believe in it as a law of natural causation, though, as we all know, a variant of it forms the basis of a system of medicine which still flourishes among us. Such positive knowledge as we possess concerning the psychological processes underlying the blend of medicine and magic leads us into no mystical dawn of the human mind, but introduces us to concepts and beliefs of the same order as those which direct our own social activities.

2

In the first chapter I dealt especially with the relations between medicine and magic, using the latter term for two kinds of processes: that in which disease is ascribed to direct human agency, and that in which the methods of treatment involve no element of appeal to higher powers, in spite of the fact that disease is ascribed to the action of spiritual beings.

PROCESSES OF DIAGNOSIS AND PROGNOSIS

It may have been noted that little was said about the processes of diagnosis and prognosis. Although the nature of the belief in causation directly determines the mode of treatment, the discovery of the cause usually needs no special rite. It is inferred immediately by the patient or his friends from their knowledge of acts, on the part of the patient, which would have offended a man or spirit believed to have the power of inflicting disease.

Where definite rites are performed for the purpose of diagnosis these often have a religious character, even where the treatment appears to be entirely of a magical order. Thus, in Murray Island, in Torres Straits, disease is believed to occur by the action of certain men who, through their possession of objects called *zogo* and their knowledge of the appropriate rites, have the power of inflicting disease. Thus, one *zogo* is believed to make people lean and hungry and at the same time to produce dysentery; another will produce constipation, and a third insanity.

When anyone falls ill the patient may know at once whom he has offended, so that no special process of diagnosis is necessary, but often the patient or his friends have recourse to certain men who own a shrine called *tomog zogo*, where a process of divination is carried out. This shrine consists of a number of stones and shells arranged so as to form an irregular plan of the island.[1] The place is visited at daybreak by those who have special knowledge. If a lizard comes out of one of the shells, the house or village which that shell represents will indicate the abode of the person by whom the sickness has been produced. If two lizards come from different shells and fight, the shell from which the victorious lizard has emerged would represent the abode of the sorcerer. This shrine was also consulted for the purpose of prognosis, a dead lizard being a sign of the death of the patient. Various other forms of divination are practised. In Murray Island, and still more in the western islands of the Torres Straits, the skulls of relatives are used for this purpose, the ghost to whom the skull belonged in life giving the desired information in a dream.[2]

In the case of the *tomog zogo* of Murray Island we do not know enough of the attitude towards the animals who provide the material for diagnosis to enable us to say how far the process can be called religious, but the reference to the skulls of ancestors, which takes place in these and other islands of Torres Straits, certainly belongs to the category of religion, forming part of a religious cult of ancestors.

---

[1] *Report Cambridge Expedition to Torres Straits*, vi, 1908, p. 261.
[2] *Ibid.*, v, p. 362, and vi, p. 266.

The cult of ancestors is still more definite in Melanesia. In many parts of that ethnographic province this cult provides an example of religion of a relatively high order, in which the elements of supplication and propitiation are clearly present. It may be noted that, here again, the appeal to the ghosts of ancestors may take place for the purpose of diagnosis in rites which have otherwise a definitely magical character.

Methods of prognosis are even more apt to have a purely religious character. Thus, when a chief in the island of Ambrim in the New Hebrides is gravely ill, little seems to be done by way of treatment; but the son or brother of the sick man takes a pig to a heap of stones called *worwor*, which had been built when the chief acquired his rank. After killing the pig on the *worwor* it is left there as a gift for the ghosts of the chief's ancestors. That night the ghost of the father of the sick man will talk to his son or brother in his sleep, and will say whether the sick man will or will not recover. In the latter case, the people may not be content with the adverse prognosis, but will kill a second pig of a kind more valuable than the first, in the hope of obtaining a more favourable answer. At the same time prayer is offered to the ancestor to allow the sick man to stay with his friends. The only treatment employed is to rub the sick man, but this is evidently of little account beside the strictly religious practices of divination by dream and of prayer, by which the people seek to discover, and, if need be, attempt to avert a fatal result.

It is, I think, a matter of interest that the aid of superhuman or divine powers should show itself so definitely in connexion with prognosis. It is instructive that this difficult and uncertain art should, in such a people as the Melanesians, bring out more clearly than any other aspect of their leechcraft the close interdependence of medicine and religion.

DISEASE ATTRIBUTED TO INFRACTION OF TABOO

The close relation between the practice of medicine and the cult of the dead ancestors exists all through Melanesia, but probably the combined rites have nowhere reached a greater pitch of elaboration than in the western islands of the British Solomons, where the subject was carefully studied by Mr. A. M. Hocart and myself some years ago. (I am greatly indebted to Mr. Hocart for his permission to publish this preliminary extract from our joint work.)

In the little island of Mandegusu or Eddystone, where Mr. Hocart and I spent several months, we found between the treatment of disease and certain religious practices, especially that of taboo, a connexion so intimate that the account of medical practice is at the same time an account of taboo. The relation between the two is so close that it would be impossible to deal with one independently of the other. Nearly every disease which occurs in this little island is ascribed to the infraction of a taboo on the fruit of certain trees, especially the coconut and betel-vine, the taboo, as well as the sign by which it is known, being called *kenjo*. The process of *kenjo* has a large number of varieties, each variety being the property of a man or small group of men, the right to practise being acquired, partly by purchase from, partly through instruction by, one already in possession of the art. The knowledge thus acquired concerns a number of rites, one carried out when the taboo is imposed, another when it is removed, and still another to allow fruit taken from tabooed trees to be used. In addition, a number of rites are learnt, by means of which to cure or ameliorate the disease which falls on one who uses fruit from the tabooed trees without the performance of the rites which should accompany its removal. Each of these rites has a special name, *salanga* being that used for the therapeutic process. With certain exceptions, all belong to the same man or group of men. Thus, it is only a man who is able to impose or remove the taboo who is able to treat the disease produced by its infraction, and, as we shall see shortly, there is a close resemblance between the rites connected with the process of taboo and those of the more strictly medical kind. Mr. Hocart and I found about a hundred examples of such conjoined processes of taboo and medicine, and obtained a record of more than sixty. The following is an example of one of these processes, namely, that connected with the taboo called kirengge, the infraction of which produces epilepsy and other convulsive seizures.

The sign of the kenjo is put up on or by the side of the tree or trees to be tabooed, and consists of several plants, the number of leaves or shoots of each plant being usually four, the sacred number of the island. The taboo sign of kirengge also includes a stone and a coral, both of which irritate the skin when touched, as well as the butterfly called kirengge, the common use of this word for the butterfly and epilepsy being due to the resemblance between the movements of the insect and those of the disease.

The leaves and other objects are put in a forked stick by the side of the tree to be protected with the following formula:—

"This is yours, ye spirits of the kenjo; this yours, ye four old women, four old women who knew the kenjo. Ye four old women in Mbakia, be favourable. Noemali, be favourable. Kiambakia, Tupombakia, Saemali, Mbukumenia. Grant my prayer against the man who steals the kenjo. Ye two lipa, grant my prayer." The proper names mentioned in this formula are those of dead women, who once knew the process, while the fifth is that of a special tomate or ghost, the tomate kirengge, apparently a personification of epilepsy, derived perhaps from some dead man who suffered from the disease. The lipa is a special kind of fish.

If the owner of the tree wishes to use any of its fruit, four sprigs of a plant called nyou are swept over the fruit with the words, "I sweep it down to throw it away. Do not return to this man. Go away to thy mother; go away to thy father. Go away."

These words indicate that some influence is thus removed from the fruit, and there is reason to believe that this influence is that of the *tomate* or ghost by whom epilepsy is believed to be produced.

If it is desired to remove the taboo altogether from the tree, the leaves and other objects making up the *kenjo* sign are thrown away in some unfrequented spot, so that there is no danger that it shall be trodden upon, a proceeding which is believed to have fatal results. When the *kenjo* is removed, the following formula is uttered: "Depart and go to the sky, do not remain on earth, thou spirit of the *kenjo*. Depart. Be cooled in the fresh water. Depart, looking to the sun; depart, looking at the sky; go up and adhere to the thunder that sounds in the sky. Go back, not to return. Depart."

When anyone suffers from epilepsy or other convulsive seizure which is recognized as *kirengge*, he and his friends consult one known to have the power of imposing the *kenio kirengge*.

This man visits the patient and strokes him from the head downwards with four leaves called *nyou*, some moss, soot and scrapings of wood, uttering the formula: "Stroke away. Stroke down and away. Cease thou. Let the man live; do not return. They have given me a good ring." The last clause of this formula, and two in that used in removing the taboo refer to the fee, the chief money of the island consisting of arm-rings. The patient is then fumigated with the smoke of certain leaves, and the patient sniffs the smoke while the leech utters over him the words: "Be favourable, thou ancient woman. Thou new spirit. Ye four ancient women." Leaves are then put round the neck of the patient with the words, "Be favourable, thou. Favour this man. Let him live." A fillet is then put round the head of the patient, and a girdle of leaves over his shoulder, with the words, "Be favourable and let the fits cease." After saying these words the leech leaves the patient, and goes away without looking back. This treatment is carried out on the last four days of the waning moon. It is performed on two successive days; then a day is left for the spirit or spirits of the *kenjo* to work, and then on the fourth day the rites are again performed, this setting aside of the third day for the action of the higher powers being a regular feature of the *salanga* process of a *kenjo*. At the end of four months the whole process is repeated.

At the end of the treatment four small puddings are burnt on a fire by the leech with the words, "Here is the pudding for you, the spirit of *kirengge*. Be favourable. Let this man go. Let me not return hereafter." Four other puddings are put in the thatch of the patient's house.

THE RELIGIOUS ELEMENT

The religious element in these rites is obvious. The note of supplication runs through all the formulas, which can definitely be regarded as prayers to beings who have the power to withhold that for which they are asked. The burnt-offering at the end of the whole proceedings has clearly a propitiatory character, and may also be regarded as a thank-offering to the ghostly being or beings through whose intervention the successful treatment has been brought about.

The special point of interest, however, in these proceedings is the intimate blending of the therapeutic process with the institution of taboo, which both in this and other parts of Melanesia has a definite religious character. Disease is held to be the result of the infraction of a taboo imposed in the name and under the sanction of the ghosts of the dead. Taking the fruit of trees so protected is not punished by the offender's fellow men, but punishment comes directly from the higher powers without any human intervention. The rites of the leech are only the means by which the help of these higher powers is obtained. They are designed to remove the misfortune which has followed the breaking of the taboo, which must be regarded as a sin rather than a crime. Though I have called the human agent a leech he might more fitly or just as fitly be regarded as a priest, whose special privilege it is to call on the higher powers to remove the penalty which the sufferer has brought upon himself by his sacrilege. Though the arm-ring given as a fee is kept by the leech, it is regarded as given to the spirits through whose activity the cure is brought about.

In addition to their beliefs in the production of disease by the ghosts who watch over tabooed trees, the natives of Eddystone Island also believe in a number of beings with special names, such as Mateana, Sea, Ilongo, Paro, Mbimbigo, to whom the power of producing disease is ascribed. These beings are personifications of natural phenomena such as thunderbolts, shooting stars, and the rainbow, and most of them have special haunts, often associated with the presence of shrines. Intrusion on these haunts is one of the causes to which disease is ascribed; but these beings are believed to inflict disease quite apart from any offence on the part of the victim. The most frequent mechanism, however, by which they are believed to produce sickness is through the breaking of a taboo. When a man falls ill with symptoms ascribed to Mateana, it is supposed that the disease has been inflicted by Mateana, owing to the infraction of a special taboo associated with this being, and called *kenjo* Mateana. It is assumed that Mateana would not have afflicted the sufferer with fever if he had not broken the taboo associated with this being. It is probable that we have here an example of fusion between two different beliefs, one in the production of disease by a personification of the thunderbolt, and another according to which disease is ascribed to a transgression of the institution of taboo.

RELIGIOUS CHARACTER ACQUIRED BY MAGICAL PROCESS

I hope to deal with this process of fusion on another occasion. All that I need point out now is that both the elements in this process of fusion are clearly of a religious character. Two sets of belief concerning the causation and treatment of disease have been unified without in any way destroying the religious character of the product of the fusion. There are, however, examples in Eddystone Island in which a similar process of fusion has given a religious character to processes for the production of disease which would otherwise fall clearly into the category of magic. Thus, the breaking of one kind of taboo exposes the transgressor to the action of one of a number of men called *njiama*, whose powers closely resemble those ascribed in many parts of the world to the evil eye. One who breaks this taboo falls ill with a set of symptoms, which are believed to show the action of a *njiama*. In some of these cases blood gushes from the mouth of the patient, who dies at once, but in slighter cases there is a definite rite of treatment which follows lines similar to those of other curative rites connected with taboos.

The infraction of another *kenjo*, *kenjo mba*, brings as its consequence a disease ascribed to the action of a sorcerer called *mba*, who is believed to produce disease by acting on a fragment of food or an object which has been used by the person on whom it is intended to inflict illness, the case thus falling into the third category of magic described in my first lecture. The action of a *mba* can take place quite independently of the breaking of a taboo, but the tendency of the people to regard disease as a punishment for sin is so strong that a sorcerer is not supposed to be able to effect his purpose unless his victim puts himself in the wrong by breaking a taboo.

The acquirement of a religious character by a process which is primarily of a magical kind shows itself in another way in connexion with the sorcery of Eddystone Island. When a person is afflicted with illness believed to be due to the action of a *mba*, the essential part of the treatment consists in the recovery of the fragment of food or other object, called *penupenu*, by means of which the sorcerer acts upon his victim. This *penupenu* may be recovered in two ways. In one the relatives of the patient go to a man reputed to have the power of divination in respect of this condition. The diviner holds up an arm-ring and recites the names of all the persons believed to possess magical powers, and when one of the names is mentioned the arm-ring begins to revolve. The person of the sorcerer having been thus revealed, the relatives visit him and accuse him of the deed. The suspected man may confess at once, and restore the hidden *penupenu* to his victim. If he refuses to confess he is suspended by one arm to the bough of a tree. As a rule a confession soon follows, but if there is long delay it is concluded that some mistake has been made in the divination by which the diagnosis was reached, and the suspended and suspected person is released. It may be noted that the patient in such a case will recover, because his mind is freed from the idea that his illness is due to the action of a sorcerer.

This mode of procedure departs from that proper to magic in the recourse to divination by the arm-ring, a process which definitely depends on the agency of an ancestral ghost. The suspension of the supposed sorcerer has the character of an ordeal, but with no obvious religious character. In the other mode of procedure in cases in which the action of a *mba* has been diagnosed, the religious character is evident. A man with especial knowledge and powers appeals to certain spirits called *tomate kuri*, who are believed to be able to find the *penupenu* in order to restore it to the sick man, the recovery of the *penupenu* being accompanied by rites similar to those by which the diseases incurred through breaking of a taboo are cured.

The religious character of the medical art is thus so strong in Eddystone Island that procedures which are primarily of the same order as the magic of other places are both diagnosed and treated by means involving the supplication and propitiation of the spirits of the dead, who are the chief objects of the religious rites of the people. There seems to have been in action a process of unification whereby the most diverse modes of regarding disease, modes which clearly belong to wholly different categories elsewhere, have been brought under one head in respect of diagnosis and treatment. The same holds good to a certain extent of the beliefs in causation, in that it is held that the production of disease by human agency would not be effective unless the sufferer had rendered himself liable to such maleficent action by his transgression of a religious ordinance.

The close relation between religion and the production and cure of disease occurs in many parts of Melanesia. Thus, in those islands which possess the institution of totemism, disease is said to follow any infraction of totemic ordinances, such as killing or eating the totem. Since these ordinances have the nature of taboos, we are again brought into contact with the relation between medicine and taboo. In the New Hebrides, where taboo is especially associated with certain complex organizations in which men rise from rank to rank by the killing of pigs, the transgression of these taboos brings sickness in its train. This religious character of leechcraft does not, however, stand alone in Melanesia, but is often accompanied by magical practices of the most definite kind. In some places, as in the Banks and Torres Islands, and probably in New Britain and New Ireland, these take the most important place in the lives and thoughts of the people. In other parts the religious aspect of leechcraft is predominant, and, as we have already seen in Eddystone Island, this predominance may be so great that magic may become altogether subordinated to that view of disease according to which it is regarded as a punishment for sin.

INDEPENDENT OCCURRENCE OF DISEASE

I must now consider briefly those cases in which disease is believed to arise independently of any action on the part of human beings or of higher powers. This belief exists in many parts of Melanesia and New Guinea, and is probably universal, though it has attracted little notice beside the more striking customs which show the relation of leechcraft with magic and religion.

The diseases thus regarded are such as we are accustomed to group together as "minor ailments". It is especially when disease appears to threaten life that people begin to think of human or spiritual agency. As among ourselves, these "minor ailments" are largely treated without the aid of any specialized practitioners, and by measures which correspond with our domestic remedies. Thus, Professor Seligman tells us[1] that, among the Sinaugolo of New Guinea, a sorcerer is only consulted when ordinary treatment has been found of no avail.

In some cases the beliefs which underlie the treatment of the grave examples of disease are also concerned in the treatment of these minor ailments. Thus, in Eddystone Island, certain sores on the limbs which are believed to "come of themselves" are yet treated by measures similar to those employed in diseases ascribed to the infraction of a taboo, and one such treatment is accompanied by a burnt-offering to spiritual beings, which offering forms a feature of the curative rites of a taboo.

Because certain cases of disease are not ascribed to direct human or spiritual agency, we must not conclude that they therefore fall within the domain of what we should call "natural" causation. If we inquire into the beliefs concerning the causation of these minor ailments in such a place as Eddystone Island, we are told that they are believed to come of themselves

---

[1] Journ. Anth. Inst., 1902, xxxii, p. 300.

and are not, therefore, the occasion of rites such as naturally follow disease ascribed to the neglect of religious injunctions. It would seem that these diseases attract little attention, and do not afford material for speculation. It is true that many of the troubles thus believed to "come of themselves" are common and a source of great discomfort, though, as a rule, they do not threaten life. It is a question whether it is not their very frequency which takes them out of the magical and religious spheres. It is the exceptional, or at any rate the less habitual, incidents of life that tend to excite the speculations of mankind,[1] and occurrences so frequent in the tropics as the outbreak of sores on the limbs tend to remain without the circle of medico-religious interest, just as our own colds and other habitual ailments remain to a large extent without the scope of our own medicine.

VARIETY IN LEECHCRAFT

The belief in the occurrence of disease independently of human or spiritual agency introduces an element of variety into the leechcraft of savage peoples. Even when it is decided that some human or spiritual agency has been at work, there may still remain ample scope for variety in the treatment adopted. If we can judge by the following experience in Eddystone Island, such peoples as the Melanesians put their faith in many doctors, and are not content with one physician or one remedy.

A man who had acted as one of our assistants in this island fell ill with apical pneumonia. After he had been ill for a few days I heard that he was anxious to be treated by me, and I attended him for the rest of his illness. He was already being treated by a noted leech of the island, Kundakolo, to whom I owe much of my knowledge of Eddystone medicine. On one of my later visits

[1] Cf. W. H. R. Rivers, *Folk Lore*, 1912, xxiii, p. 307.

another of our assistants, also a noted leech, who went with me, carried out a course of treatment consisting of rubbings, spittings, and prayers as soon as I had finished my interview, his treatment being designed to remedy the sweating which was at that time the chief cause of complaint. I thus knew during my attendance on the patient that I had two rivals in my art, but it was only after the patient had recovered that we learnt there had been at least a dozen. The first diagnosis had been that the patient was suffering from sorcery, or *mba*, and three different leeches were called upon in succession to carry out different forms of treatment for this condition. I then began my visits, but at the same time two other practitioners were called in, who performed two other "cures" for sorcery. The diagnosis of *mba* was then given up, this being about the time of the crisis, and a woman then carried out the treatment for *njiama*, on the supposition that the patient had fallen under the spell of the evil eye. This was followed by a treatment assigned to cure a symptom ascribed to a being named Ave, whom we shall meet again shortly. This was followed by three separate "cures" for a condition called *tagosoro*, usually produced by the action of the beings called Mateana and Sea. As these were not wholly successful, the original diagnosis of *mba* was made the basis of the next treatment. A month later the patient was considering whether he would not call in another practitioner to treat him again for *tagosoro*, on account of his failure to recover his strength completely. At one stage of illness, when the patient was delirious and insisted on walking about naked, his friends had considered the propriety of calling in a practitioner skilled in the treatment for the infraction of *kenjo tuturu*, which has as a result a condition of insanity ascribed to beings, called *tuturu*, who live in the bush.

DIFFERENTIATION OF LEECH FROM PRIEST

The high degree of specialization of medical function which exists in Eddystone Island may serve as an introduction to a subject I have until now left on one side. In the first chapter I stated that one of the means by which it is possible to distinguish medicine from magic and religion is an inquiry how far the leech is differentiated from the sorcerer and the priest. In the area with which I am specially dealing in these lectures, it may be said at once that there is little evidence of such differentiation. In Australia, New Guinea, and Melanesia it would seem that the simpler remedies, of which I spoke just now, may be used by anyone, there being in this respect no differentiation of the leech from the general body of the people. Those who combine the practice of medicine with that of magical or religious rites usually acquire their art by a special process, either of initiation or instruction, and in Melanesia such knowledge has always to be purchased. The most complete instruction in any branch of medico-magical or medico-religious art is of no avail to the pupil unless money has passed from himself to his instructor. This instruction and purchase, however, nearly always include both the production and cure of disease, where disease is ascribed to human agency, and the power and knowledge to perform rites other than those of a curative nature where medicine is allied with religion.

In Eddystone Island, however, a distinct step has been taken towards the differentiation of the leech from the priest. A man who buys the knowledge which enables him to impose a taboo necessarily buys at the same time the knowledge of the process by means of which to treat the illness which follows infraction of the taboo. It does not follow, however, that he uses this part of his knowledge. Certain men of the island have acquired a special reputation for success in the application of remedies, such men being called *tinoni salanga*. In these *tinoni salanga* we have clearly present the beginning of the differentiation of the leech from the priest. It may be interesting to mention some of the conditions which seem to have brought about this distinction. One is that a *tinoni salanga* who wishes his treatment to be successful should use a special kind of shell-instrument, called a *rikerike*, with which to cut and scrape roots or other ingredients of his pharmacopœia. One who steps over this instrument angers the *tomate* or ghostly ancestor from whom the leech derives his powers, the ghost showing his anger by the infliction of illness. Owing to the danger so incurred men who have bought the knowledge of a taboo will sometimes decline to use their knowledge of the associated treatment, and leave that part of their art to others willing to take the risk. Another deterrent is the need for sexual abstinence on the part of a leech, especially in certain rites, such as those for the cure of ulcers.

There is another indication that medicine in the strict sense of the term is becoming dissociated in Eddystone Island from the religious attitude. The influence of the being called Mateana shows itself in the occurrence of fever, pain, and weakness, this complex of symptoms being called *tagosoro*. At the present time there seems to be a distinct tendency to diagnose and treat *tagosoro* as a morbid entity, independently of any belief in the anger of Mateana or the transgression of a taboo. This was probably the case in the three treatments for *tagosoro* carried out on the patient I have already mentioned, while the treatment for symptoms ascribed to Ave may also have been of a similar nature. It is possible, however, that this modification of the leechcraft of Eddystone Island is due to recent European influence. This may also be true of the movement towards specialization of the leech, for one of the first results of such external influence is to lower resistance to the dangers and hardships which so often accompany the religious and magical rites of savage man.

It must be noted that the widespread failure to distinguish the leech from the sorcerer or priest is not due to any failure in the specialization of medical function itself. Indeed, the matter is rather the other way. Such people as the Papuan or Melanesian have carried the differentiation of medical function in some respects to a far higher pitch than even we have reached in our highly specialized medical art. In Eddystone Island the treatment of different diseases is so highly specialized that one man will treat rheumatism, another fever, a third epilepsy, and a fourth insanity, although in each case the cure of disease is intimately associated with certain religious functions. An example of similar specialization in Torres Straits has already been given in this lecture, and still another example is found in the island of Tami on the north-eastern coast of New Guinea, where one man knows how to cure pain in the chest, another pain in the abdomen, a third rheumatism, and a fourth catarrh.[1] Specialism is thus present in a pre-eminent degree; but this specialism has taken a direction which has probably been antagonistic to the development of that kind of differentiation of social function which among ourselves, after centuries of progress, has made medicine a wholly independent department of social life.

EPIDEMIC DISEASE

A few special points remain for consideration. I have so far treated disease as if it were a condition which only affects individuals, and have said nothing of those cases of disease in which a whole population or a large portion of it suffers simultaneously from disease. I have now to consider what is the attitude of the peoples we are considering towards epidemic disease.

Here, as in individual cases of disease, we find medicine intimately blended with magic or religion. Among these peoples whose lives are dominated by magic, epidemics are ascribed to

---

[1] In Neuhauss, *Deutsch Neu-Guinea*, iii, 516.

the action of sorcerers, but it is supposed that they are produced by the sorcery of members of some other village or some other island. I have recorded[1] a case from the Banks Islands, in which a man, who wished to injure a woman who had refused to marry him, held a bamboo containing certain ingredients so that the wind should carry its influence to the island where the woman was living. An epidemic illness which shortly followed was ascribed to his action. Payment was made to the sorcerer, who sent young coconuts to which he had imparted power (*mana*), and the milk of these coconuts was poured at the door of every sufferer, so that the epidemic might be stayed.

For an example of epidemic disease ascribed to the agency of higher powers, I may return to Eddystone Island. Here such disease is supposed to be due to the action of a being or beings, called Ave, whose coming is indicated by the presence of broken rainbows, shooting stars, red clouds, and showers of fine rain while the sun is shining. The symptoms of the disease usually produced by Ave are fever, headache, and cough. The Ave probably were spirits or ghosts associated with certain neglected shrines in Eddystone. Dysentery epidemics are ascribed to Ave from Ysabel.

When an epidemic ascribed to Ave visits the island the people appeal to one who knows the appropriate rites. This man, with certain companions, visits a now disused village. After uttering the names of certain ghosts, probably those of his predecessors in the knowledge of the rite, he proceeds: "You, at the root of the sky, come down and depart. There is an end of the men; there is an end of the chiefs; an end of the chiefs' wives; an end of the chiefs' children. Come and depart thou, etc.," the prayer ending with an exclamation like a bark, when all present shout. Then the root of turmeric is distributed, and all chew it and spit it about the path as they go towards the shore, making as much

---

[1] *The History of Melanesian Society*, i, p. 158.

noise as possible, with the idea of driving away the Ave. When they reach the shore the leader in the ceremony folds a large leaf so as to make it like a canoe. In this imitation vessel he puts ashes, some of the leaf used in thatching a house, and five small shell ornaments called *ovala*. He then utters the following words: "You! Go to Ysabel; go to Choiseul (neighbouring islands). Do not stay in Mandegusu." The canoe is then taken out to sea and put on the waves, so that it goes away from the island. It is believed to carry the Ave back to the place whence it came.

RELATIONS OF ECONOMICAL AND JURIDICAL NATURE

The chief object of this discussion has been to show the intimate relation of medicine with magic and religion among certain peoples who rank low in the scale of general culture. It may have been noticed that this tie carries with it other relations of an economical and juridical kind. Thus, the *kenjo* of Eddystone Island is not merely an example of an intimate blend between medicine and religion, but at the same time it involves the institution of private property. The people of Eddystone Island form a good example of communism in goods, large groups of persons owning land and certain other property in common. The process called *kenjo*, which we have so far studied in its relation to the social categories of medicine and religion, is also a means by which certain kinds of property—namely the fruit of certain trees—are kept for the special use of individual persons. It is a social practice by which a communistic people have progressed some way along the path of individualism.

The *kaia* rites of the Gazelle Peninsula and the Duke of York Island, which I described in the first chapter, afford another example of a similar process. The half-snake, half-human being called *kaia* is believed to abstract the soul of any person who takes fruit from the trees of the district it inhabits, persons from other districts being specially prone to suffer from its action. It is probable that the belief in the efficacy of this being is definitely fostered by the inhabitants of a district, as a means of protecting their property from the people of neighbouring districts. It would be very wrong to regard the institutions of the Solomon Islands and New Britain as inventions of the people in the interests of private property. The belief in the production of disease as a punishment for theft, however, provides a motive which tends to perpetuate the ideas and practices which bring medicine into so intimate a relation with religion. We have here only one of countless examples showing that among peoples of rude culture the distinction of social categories from one another is far more difficult than among ourselves. The religious character of the medical art among such peoples is only one example of the way in which religion and the religious attitude permeate every part of their social life. Religion among such people is not a matter for one day in the week, but influences every act of their daily lives.

THE PART PLAYED BY SUGGESTION

Another subject well illustrated by the proceedings described in this book is the evidence concerning the part played by suggestion in the production and cure of diseases among such people as the Papuans and Melanesians. There can be no question that such processes as I have recorded here are efficacious. Men who have offended one whom they believe to have magical powers sicken, and even die, as the direct result of their belief; and if the process has not gone too far they will recover if they can be convinced that the spell has been removed. Similarly, one who has intruded on the haunt of a ghost or spirit will suffer, it may be, fatal illness, because he believes that he has lost his soul; and he will recover after the performance of rites to which he ascribes the power of restoring the lost soul to his body.

Doubtless, with this real factor of suggestion there is mixed up much deception, especially on the part of those to whose special knowledge the production and cure of disease is ascribed. If one falls ill with symptoms which by popular belief are ascribed to a sorcerer, or to some spirit whose influence is believed to be under the power of a priest, the sorcerer or priest is only too ready to accept the rôle ascribed to him to earn money and at the same time enhance his reputation for medico-magical or medico-religious powers.

At the same time there is reason to believe that he is not wholly a deceiver, but in some measure shares the general belief in his own powers. Even that degree of intimacy with those who practise medico-magical and medico-religious arts which is possible to such a visitor as I have been among several peoples, is enough to show the sincerity and earnestness of many of these practitioners. I believe that, in many cases, it is the same among ourselves, and that a study of our own quacks and charlatans, with that amount of care which we devote to the Australian or the Melanesian leech, would show us the impostor far less than is usually supposed. Imposition there is, no doubt, but, if such a study were carried out from a psychological point of view, it would often reveal the enthusiast and the crank in even greater measure than the impostor.

Not only will the study of peoples of rude culture help us to estimate aright the part taken by fraud and deception in certain forms of the medical art of the civilized world, but, what is far more important, it will help us also to understand better the place taken by suggestion both in the production and the treatment of disease. From the psychological point of view the difference between the rude arts I have described in this book and much of our own medicine is not one of kind, but only of degree.

RATIONALITY OF THE LEECHCRAFT

The chief lesson, however, impressed upon us by the facts brought forward here, is one the importance of which reaches far beyond the limits of our special subject. This lesson is the rationality of the leechcraft of such peoples as the Papuan and the Melanesian. The practices of these peoples in relation to disease are not a medley of disconnected and meaningless customs, but are inspired by definite ideas concerning the causation of disease. Their modes of treatment follow directly from their ideas concerning etiology and pathology. From our modern standpoint we are able to see that these ideas are wrong. But the important point is that, however wrong may be the beliefs of the Papuan and Melanesian concerning the causation of disease, their practices are the logical consequence of those beliefs.

We may say even that these peoples practise an art of medicine which is in some respects more rational than our own, in that its modes of diagnosis and treatment follow more directly from their ideas concerning the causation of disease. According to the opinion of the civilized world, these ideas of causation are wrong, or contain but grains of truth here and there; but once grant these ideas, and the body of medical practice follows therefrom with a logical consistency which it may take us long to emulate in our pursuit of a medicine founded upon the sciences of physiology and psychology.

I tried to show, in the first chapter, that the concepts underlying the magical procedure of savage man have not the vague and indefinite character often assigned to them, but form clear and relatively concrete motives for the complex procedures of the sorcerer and leech. These concepts form the starting-point of his logical processes, and the general conclusion which can, I believe, be drawn from the facts before us, is that these logical processes are as definite as the premises from which they start.

There can be no greater hindrance to progress in our attempts to understand the mind of the man of lowly culture than the belief so widely held, that his actions are determined by motives having that vague and lawless character ascribed by many to the thought of savage man. There are even those who hold that such peoples as the Papuan and Melanesian have not yet reached the logical stage of thought.[1] I believe there is no single department of social life in which it cannot be shown that this view is false. I have elsewhere attempted a demonstration of its falsity in one department of social life.[2] I hope the facts brought forward here are sufficient to show that, in the department of his activity in which he endeavours to cope with disease, savage man is no illogical or prelogical creature, but that his actions are guided by reasoning as definite as that which we can claim for our own medical practices.

It must be noted, however, that the examples of leechcraft which have been recorded in this book have not always formed part of a strictly logical and consistent system. An instance from Eddystone Island is the way in which the causation of disease by such agencies as Mateana and Sea, as well as by the evil eye and sorcery, has become subservient to the ancestor-cult which underlies the kenjo. The indefiniteness of the beliefs connected with the being called Ave gives another instance from the same island. As an example from New Guinea may be mentioned the employment, by the Kai, of several remedies, such as bleeding and massage, which do not, so far as we know, immediately follow from their ideas concerning the causation of disease. Such cases lead us to a set of problems which I have left on one side in this book, problems which would lead us to a mode of studying early medicine too large to be included in the scope of this course of lectures—namely, the study of the transformations suffered by medical beliefs and practices as the result of the

---

[1] Lévy-Bruhl, *Les Fonctions Mentales dans les Sociétés Inférieures*, Paris, 1910.
[2] "The Primitive Conception of Death," *Hibbert Journal*, 1912, x, p. 393.

contact and blending of peoples. I have dealt with two only of the methods by which social facts may be studied—the sociological and the psychological. I must leave the far more difficult problem of the historical relations of medicine, magic, and religion for another occasion.

3

In the previous chapters I have been dealing with the relations between medicine, magic, and religion descriptively, and from the sociological and psychological points of view. I showed that, in Melanesia and New Guinea, which I chose as the region to illustrate my subject, there is an intimate connexion between three sets of social process, which are clearly distinguished from one another by ourselves and other civilized peoples. I dealt briefly with some of the psychological factors underlying the union between three kinds of process, but left altogether on one side any consideration of the mechanisms by which the relations between medicine, magic, and religion had come into being, and those by which processes so closely related in one part of the world had elsewhere become distinct and self-contained departments of social life. I have chosen this historical and evolutionary treatment for the second half of this book.

EVOLUTION OF SOCIAL CUSTOMS AND INSTITUTIONS

I must begin by considering briefly the general problem

concerning the nature of the evolutionary process in its relation to the history of human society. The practice of medicine is a social process, subject to the same laws, and to be studied by the same methods as other social processes. The chief aim of this book is, by means of the relations between medicine, magic, and religion, to illustrate the principles and methods which should guide and direct the study of the history of social institutions.

INDEPENDENT EVOLUTION

If I had been writing only a few years ago my mode of treatment would have been very simple. At that time, in common with most students of human society, I believed that, after a dispersal widely over the earth, which had taken place at an epoch so distant as to place its study almost without the range of practical science, mankind had evolved his customs and institutions with a high, even in some cases a complete, degree of independence. When I found close similarity of custom or belief in widely separated places, I was content to ascribe it to a process of independent evolution, the course of which had been determined by the tendency of the human mind to respond in certain uniform ways to the action of its physical and social environment. I should have been content with the position, that the close relation of medicine to magic and religion which, in Chapters 1 and 2, I endeavoured to demonstrate for Melanesia and New Guinea, represents only one stage in a process of differentiation whereby one kind of social activity has developed elsewhere into three distinct departments of social life. I should have held that Melanesia and New Guinea have preserved for us a stage in the evolution of human society in which this differentiation has made so little progress that it is still difficult to distinguish medicine from magic and religion, while, among ourselves, the process of differentiation has gone so far that each of the two departments which our society has preserved has its own specialized practitioners, its own code of social regulations, and its own body of beliefs concerning the relation of mankind to his surroundings.

Moreover, when comparing the pathological ideas and the diagnostic and therapeutic practices of different peoples, I should have held any similarities which became apparent to be the natural result of the unity of action of the human mind. The diseases of one part of the world are so much like those of another that I should have regarded it as the most natural thing in the world that mankind should have evolved similar beliefs concerning the nature of disease and similar practices by which to modify or neutralize its effects.

I should have explained the similarities between the beliefs and practices of medicine, and those of magic and religion, in a similar manner. I should have argued that, whether magic and religion have grown out of the beliefs and sentiments of mankind towards the mysteries of nature or towards those of his own birth, life, and death, or towards both together, these mysteries are everywhere similar in character. I should have regarded it as natural that the mind of man in the making should have reacted towards them in ways so similar as to have produced the worship of the sun and other heavenly bodies, of vegetation and of other natural forces, together with the cults of the dead which are found in so many parts of the earth. It would not have surprised me that a body of customs and beliefs embodying the reaction of mankind towards the appearances of nature, or of his own life, should be closely connected with those embodying his attitude towards disease. If then, as now, I had given a pre-eminent degree of importance to the great mystery of death, as the most important motive in the development of the religion of mankind, the connexion of religion with the art designed to meet disease, the harbinger of death, would have seemed especially natural. I should have dwelt on the vast part which ideas connected with death and the life after death have taken in the religious development of mankind, and should have regarded the close connexion between medicine and religion as the natural consequence of the intimate relation between disease and death.

In this brief sketch of what I should have said if I had written a few years ago, there is much which I still believe to be true. That running through the history of mankind there has been in action a process of specialization of social function stands beyond all doubt, and I should have been keeping strictly within the truth in regarding the increasing distinction of medicine from magic and religion as an example of this process of specialization. There would also have been much truth in the supposition that disease and death are so closely connected that, even if the earth had been divided up into independent and self-contained departments, we should have expected much similarity in the reaction of different groups of mankind towards them. The fault I now find with the account I have just given is not so much that it is false, but that it is far from being the whole truth. It errs by giving a far too simple account of a process which has in reality been exceedingly complex.

TRANSMISSION AS A FACTOR IN HUMAN CULTURE

The great change which has taken place[1] in our ideas concerning the value of such a scheme of evolution as I have sketched is due to several causes. I have time to-day only to mention one. This is that until recently far too little attention has been paid to the influences of degeneration in the history of human society. At

[1] [In his Presidential address to the Section of Anthropology at the meeting of the British Association for the Advancement of Science (see *Proceedings* for 1911), Dr. Rivers has given an account of his change of attitude, which really initiated the new movement in ethnology, which the present book does so much to illuminate. Compare also chapter vi ("The Aims of Ethnology") of his book *Psychology and Politics* (1923).]

one time the savage and barbarous cultures of mankind were universally regarded as examples of degeneration, but with the general acceptance of the doctrine of evolution, degeneration was forgotten or neglected. In accordance with the general course of the progress of knowledge an idea, which had till then been dominant, was thrust aside; and even the many cases where degeneration in human society is obvious were ignored or held to be of little account. As one among many examples of this neglect, I may mention that students were led to attach great importance to the rude means of navigation now found on many parts of the earth. The possibility that this rude condition may have been the result of degeneration was neglected. It was concluded that voyages on the sea had taken no appreciable part in the early wanderings of mankind. Since, in the absence of communication by sea, the existing connexions between the different continents are insufficient to explain the present distribution of mankind, ancient land connexions were assumed, thus putting back the dispersal of mankind to so remote a date as to leave ample scope for processes of independent development. It is only necessary to show that the art of navigation might not only degenerate but even disappear,[1] and voyages by sea again enter into our schemes[2] of the early peopling of the earth, thus bringing transmission out of the lumber-room into which it had been cast by most students of human society.

Once we acknowledge transmission as an important factor in the history of human culture, once we appreciate the important part taken by degeneration[3] in this history, many old problems can be seen in quite a new light. When we find a mode of

[1] W. H. Rivers, "The Disappearance of Useful Arts", *Festschrift tillegnad Edvard West-ermarck*, Helsingfors, 1912, p. 109.

[2] G. Elliot Smith, "Ancient Mariners," *Report and Proceedings of the Belfast Natural History and Philosophical Society*, Session 1916–17, p. 46.

[3] [This theme has been elaborated in W. J. Perry's book, *The Children of the Sun* (1923).]

treating disease closely related to a magical or religious practice, it becomes possible that the relation does not represent a stage in a process whereby medicine is gradually being differentiated from magic or religion, but the process may be rather one of assimilation. A therapeutic practice, devoid of any magical or religious character in its original home, may acquire this character when introduced elsewhere. The magical or religious guise thus obtained by a therapeutic practice would, in such a case, be due to the prominence of magic or religion in the culture of the people among whom the practice has been introduced. On the other hand, a magical or religious practice may have aspects which, to a people who possess a genuine art of medicine, suggest therapeutic or hygienic applications. These may lead to its becoming part of the medical art of its new home, and to the complete disappearance of its magical or religious character. In each case the relation of medicine with magic or religion is due to a process of assimilation, whereby an introduced practice has been endowed by the people who have adopted it with the features characteristic of their own culture.

Instead of human culture presenting us with a simple process of direct evolution, we have a highly complex process of interaction between peoples and their cultures, producing blended products, in the case before us, blends of medicine with magic and religion, which need new methods of inquiry and long years of patient study before the exact nature of the process, the whole instead of the partial truth, can be attained.

RELATIONS OF MEDICINE, MAGIC, AND RELIGION IN VARIOUS COUNTRIES

In the preceding chapters I dealt with a limited area, with Melanesia and New Guinea, and even then I attempted no full survey, but was content to pick out a few salient examples to illustrate the relations of medicine with magic or religion. Before I enter on the special task of this book, I must briefly sketch the nature of the relations between medicine, magic, and religion in other parts of the world. In this survey I shall begin with the countries adjacent to Melanesia.

AUSTRALIA

Australia is characterized by the large part taken by human agency in the beliefs concerning the production of disease. According to the prevailing views, this continent is held to be the special home of magic, and there is no doubt that the Australian attitude towards disease is closely bound up with practices resembling those to which the name of magic is usually given.

It is noteworthy, however, that the form of magic most widely spread over the earth, that known as sympathetic, rarely occurs in Australia. It is exceptional in this continent to act upon some part of a person with the idea of inflicting disease upon him. The usual process by which an Australian sorcerer inflicts disease is to point at his victim a bone from a dead person. It is believed that he is able to project some morbific influence into his victim, the process resembling one of which I gave an example, from the Banks Islands, earlier in this book.

The use of part of a dead man in this process raises the question, whether the method of the Australian sorcerer comes as definitely within the sphere of magic as is usually supposed. It is possible that this and other of his methods do not depend altogether, perhaps not at all, on a belief in non-human agency. The Australians certainly believe in the production of disease through the action of spiritual beings, such as the ghosts of the dead, and especially the ghosts of certain beings to whom tradition assigns the ancestry of the social group, or the introduction of new elements of culture. Australia thus presents examples of both the chief categories of causation which are found in Melanesia, but it is a question whether the cases which, on superficial observation, seem clearly to belong to the category of magic may not be only the degenerate products of a former belief in the production of disease by spiritual beings, and especially by the ghosts of the dead.

In any case, the immediate agent to whom the Australians usually ascribe the occurrence of disease is a human being, and, in accordance with this belief, the object of the friends of a person who becomes ill is to discover and propitiate the man to whose action the disease is ascribed. The process of diagnosis is mainly or exclusively directed to discover the human agent, and the only treatment is to convince the patient that his spell has been removed. Whether disease is ascribed to human or spiritual agency, the therapeutic practice is usually based on the belief that the agent has implanted in the body of his victim some material object—a piece of bone, a crystal, or a pebble—as the vehicle of the disease. It is by the supposed extraction of such an object that the cure is effected, suction being the most frequent process by which the object is removed.

POLYNESIA

While Australia, lying on one side of Melanesia, provides, at any rate from certain points of view, an example of the relation between medicine and magic, Polynesia, lying upon the other side, shows us a striking example of the intimate relation between medicine and religion. In some parts of Polynesia magic appears to be absent and, with the exception of a few simple remedies, the cure of disease is sought by means of direct appeal to higher powers, and especially to those beings called *atua*, who are almost certainly derived from the ghosts of dead ancestors.

In this part of the world especial importance is attached to the process of prognosis, which is carried out by men who enter into conditions of trance, in which they are believed to be

possessed by the ghosts of the dead. In this condition the possessed person answers inquiries concerning the outcome of the
illness, and the friends of the patient are content to accept the fiat
thus issued, and do not seek to interfere with the result by the
employment of any therapeutic measures. Among some peoples
of Polynesia medicine can hardly be said to exist, so exclusively
do the people rely upon divine help in their attitude towards
disease. Even where definite therapeutic remedies are employed
there is often evidence that these are of recent introduction. Thus
Mariner states[1] that the Tongans looked to the gods for relief
from disease, using for this purpose rites of invocation and
sacrifice. They had learnt from the Fijians, not long before
Mariner's stay in the islands, the surgical procedures which form
almost the only measures which can be regarded as strictly
therapeutic.

In some parts of Polynesia the abstraction of blood, usually by
means of incisions and scarifications, is a favourite remedy.
Vapour and cold baths and massage are also employed as therapeutic measures, but little use is made of herbs or other internal
remedies in most parts of Polynesia. An extensive vegetable
pharmacopœia has been recorded from New Zealand, but,
according to Elsdon Best,[2] the greatest living authority on the
Maoris, this is a recent growth. Before the coming of European
influence the Maoris were content to rely mainly upon spiritual
agencies similar to those invoked by the inhabitants of other
parts of Polynesia. Such internal remedies as were used in Tonga
had been derived from Fiji.[3]

The medical practice of the Hawaiian Islands, though intimately connected with religion, contains more elements of a
medical character. David Malo,[4] a native authority, says that the

---

[1] *Tonga*, 1817, ii, p. 242.

[2] See W. H. Goldie, *Transactions of the New Zealand Institute*, xxxvii, 1904, p. 2.

[3] Mariner, *loc. cit.*

[4] *Hawaiian Antiquities*, Honolulu, 1903, p. 144.

medical treatment of the sick was a matter that belonged to the worship of the gods. The treatment was applied by a *kahuna*, or priest, but it included the administration of a number of herbs, as well as the use of the vapour bath. The religious character of the treatment is shown, however, by offerings to the gods at different stages, and when the patient was chief no medicine was ever administrated without prayer.

In parts of Polynesia there is a belief in the production of disease by human agency, and by the employment of procedures resembling the magic of other places; but beliefs of this kind are of little account beside the religious attitude. In some islands they appear to be completely absent, one island where this is certainly the case being the small Polynesian settlement of Tikopia, which lies upon the fringe of Melanesia.[1]

INDONESIA

The Malay Archipelago, now usually known as Indonesia, is of especial interest in relation to Melanesia, Polynesia, and Australia, because it is almost certain that the chief external influences which have reached these areas came by way of this archipelago. Indonesia is the seat of much recent contact with the Chinese, while before this many parts of it were saturated with Hindu influence. Probably as the result of the many influences to which it has been exposed, the medical art of Indonesia presents more variety than that of Melanesia or Polynesia. The occurrence of disease is ascribed to human agency, as well as to the activity of evil spirits, of the ghosts of ancestors and relatives, and of beings who can definitely be regarded as gods.

One of the modes in which purely human agency is believed to produce disease is by acting upon separated parts of the body,

[1] W. H. R. Rivers, *History of Melanesian Society*, Cambridge, 1914, vol. i, p. 315.

the so-called sympathetic magic; and though the evidence is not
conclusive, it would appear that this form of magic rests upon
the belief in a divisible soul-substance similar to that held by the
Kai of New Guinea.[1] In Melanesia and Australia it is sometimes
difficult to be sure whether the injurious effects which follow
the rites of a sorcerer do not depend upon the administration of
poisons. In Indonesia this use of poisons stands beyond doubt,
the most striking example being the production of a lingering
intestinal complaint, often ending fatally, by the administration
of powdered bamboo. Even when the morbid effects can confidently be ascribed to a poison, however, the utterance of incantations and other actions of the poisoner show that the process is
not far removed from magic, and the agent himself probably fails
to distinguish between measures in which he administers actual
poisons, and those in which the morbid effects are entirely due
to the belief of the victim in the magical powers of one whom he
has offended.

The belief in the production of disease by magic, however,
plays a relatively small rôle in Indonesia compared with that in
which disease is ascribed to the action of spiritual or divine
beings. One of the most frequent beliefs is that, also widely
prevalent in Melanesia, in which disease is ascribed to the
abstraction of the soul or soul-substance. It is believed that the
soul is sometimes devoured by the spirits who steal it, in which
case a fatal issue is inevitable. In other cases the soul can be
recovered by a priest, and the nature of the rites performed for
this purpose shows clearly that the beliefs of this kind come
definitely into the category of religion.

An important feature of the rites performed by a priest when
dealing with disease in the island of Nias[2] is that he makes
images of wood called *adu*, which probably represent ancestral

[1] *Vide supra*, p. 19.
[2] J. P. K. de Zwaan, *Die Heilkunde der Niasser*, Haag, 1913, pp. 52 *sqq.*

ghosts.[1] Many different kinds of *adu*, bearing special names, are made for different kinds of illness. Thus, one kind is made up when the patient is suffering from fever, with swollen feet and a sensation of heaviness in the limbs, another when fever is accompanied by nightmares, and a third when there are also pains in head and body. The *adu* are made in different forms, an important feature being that the more serious the illness the larger is the number of kinds of wood that must be used. In one case, the *adu ba mbumbu*, made when all other remedies have failed, from 50 to 1,000 images are made of as many kinds of wood as can be obtained.

An *adu* is treated in various ways. It may be hung on a tree as an offering to the evil spirit who is believed to be producing the disease, or it may be set up before the patient, or before or on the roof of his house. It may be thrown into a river, the belief in this case being that the disease has entered the *adu*, and is carried away by the stream. The disease may also be transferred from the patient by touching him with a young pig, which is then slaughtered and its blood smeared on the *adu*.

Various rites accompany the use of the *adu*. Offerings may be made to the beings to whom the action of the disease is ascribed, and in the case of the *adu ba mbumbu* the priest climbs on the roof of the patient's house to pray to the "sun-god". The patient may be isolated and his diet regulated, and he may be given remedies, such as fungi from the tree believed to be inhabited by the evil spirit to which the disease is ascribed.

In some cases the occurrence of disease is believed to affect a person because he or his relatives have committed an offence against the beings to whom the disease is ascribed, but, so far as our information goes, it appears that more often disease is

[1] [It is more likely that they represent the life-giving dragon, the *naga*, or the mythical "crocodile", which is believed to restore health by restoring the deficiency of vital substance causing the illness.—G. E. S.]

believed to come about through the will of spirit or god, independently of any sin on the part of the patient.

In addition to the measures which depend upon appeal to non-human and divine beings, remedies of the domestic order are frequently employed. This branch of medicine seems to have reached a higher degree of development than in Oceania, for these remedies are used by special practitioners, often women, called *dukun*, in the island of Nias, who use massage and various internal remedies. Though definite information is lacking, it is probable that the letting of blood by means of scarification and cupping is also the business of these practitioners.

I have dealt at some length with the medicine of Australia, Polynesia, and Indonesia, because the culture of these three areas stands in a special relation to that of Melanesia. With few exceptions the people of Melanesia, Polynesia, and Indonesia regions, sometimes known collectively as Austronesia, speak languages which belong to closely related families, and have many other practices in common. We should therefore expect to find the similarity in their medical arts, and in the relation of these to magic and religion, which we have seen actually to exist. I must deal with the medicine of other parts of the world more briefly.

INDIA

Corresponding with its advanced civilization, we find in India an extensive pharmacopœia and a surgery from which that of Europe has taken more than one lesson. The practice of rhinoplasty was borrowed from India, while the first performance of surgical operations under hypnotism was largely due to the experience of this practice gained by Esdaile in this country.

Even this relatively advanced art, however, seems to have greatly degenerated from that which belonged to Indian medicine about the fifth century A.D., the degeneration apparently being due to the gradual preponderence of an old indigenous art over one introduced and developed by an immigrant people. Even at its best times, however, the close relation of medicine with religion was shown by the special practice of the medical art by members of the priestly Brahminic caste. At the present time the frequent use of formulas when remedies are administered shows clearly how close is the alliance between medicine and religion, even among the more highly civilized sections of the Indian population.

Among the less advanced sections of the community the connexion between medicine and religion is still more definite. The folk medicine of India at the present time is chiefly based on the belief that disease depends upon possession by a spirit, and the historians of Indian medicine speak of possession as characteristic of its earliest stage.

When disease is ascribed to possession the rational remedy is to rid the patient of that by which he is possessed, and, as we should expect, rites of exorcism are very prominent in Indian medicine and religion. In India we also meet the idea of disease as a punishment for sin, the beings who thus inflict disease when offended including both ghosts of ancestors and gods.

Not only is a disease believed to fall upon man as a punishment for offences which he has committed in his present life, but the doctrine of transmigration has brought with it the belief that disease may occur as punishment for offences committed in a former existence, and that they are to be remedied by the performance of religious penances.

One people of India, the Todas, whose culture is in many ways peculiar, exhibit an interesting phase in the specialization of medicine and religion. There is a definite distinction between the priest and the leech, together with a close similarity in the formulas of the therapeutic measures of the one, and the divinatory and religious rites of the other.[1]

---

[1] W. H. R. Rivers, *The Todas*, London, 1906, p. 271.

CHINA AND JAPAN

China presents us with an example of medicine which resembles in many respects that of our own Middle Ages. The main doctrine upon which Chinese medicine rests is that disease depends on disturbance of the normal equilibrium between the blood, the humours, and the life-spirit. The chief element in the system of diagnosis is a highly elaborate examination of the pulse.

On the therapeutic side there is a very extensive pharmacopœia, one writer alone enumerating no less than 1,892 remedies. Animal substances are frequently used, while the moxa, acupuncture, and massage are employed with great frequency.

The medicine of Japan is largely borrowed from China, and presents very similar characteristics; but was placed on a more rational basis by a number of physicians from the sixteenth century onwards.

AFRICA

In Africa, as in the parts of the world already considered, disease is ascribed to both human and spiritual agency, but several African peoples show a belief in the production of disease by natural causes to a far greater extent than in Austronesia.

The belief in human agency usually takes the form of sympathetic magic, depending on the belief that disease can be brought upon a man by acting upon some part of him. This belief in magic is especially prominent in West Africa, and is probably more characteristic of the Negro than of the Bantu.

Several kinds of spiritual beings are believed to inflict disease, but the ghosts of the dead seem to be the most important. In some places a distinction is made between the ghosts of ordinary people and those of chiefs or kings. There is also found the belief in special gods connected with disease, and, as in other parts of the world, it is epidemic disease which is especially ascribed to these deities.

The most frequent way in which disease is inflicted takes the form of possession, but the belief in the causation of disease by the absence of the soul or of the life-principle occurs in West Africa.

The motives which are believed to lead ghosts or other spiritual agents to inflict disease are usually the breaking of a taboo, or the neglect to make offerings, tend graves, or perform the rites which the spirits believe to be their due. If the relatives of an orphan do not give the child the social position which belongs to it, it is believed that the ghost of the child's father may inflict disease upon them.

In cases where disease is ascribed to possession by a spirit the natural remedy is exorcism, which is effected either by direct appeal to the spirit or deity, but more frequently by means of a power believed to belong to an object prepared in certain ways, the fetich which is so characteristic of African culture that the term "fetichism" has come to be widely but loosely applied to the whole of African religion. A frequent form of fetich is the horn of an ox filled with various substances to which virtue is imparted by certain rites. Another frequent mode of treatment is to carry out rites designed to transfer the disease, or rather the spirit causing the disease, to some object, such as a tree or animal, or to another human being. In the last case the spirit of the disease is believed to pass into a model of the patient in clay, which has been in contact with the patient's body. The object so animated is then put by the roadside or some other place, where it will enter the body of the next passer-by.[1] This method closely resembles the form of magic, in which a sorcerer inflicts disease upon an enemy; but differs from it in that the African purpose need not be malicious, but disease is

[1] J. Roscoe, *The Baganda*, London, 1911, p. 344.

brought upon the passer-by in the interest of one who is already ill.

In some cases in which the occurrence of disease follows an offence, such as adultery on the part of a woman while bearing or nursing a child, it is believed that the disease can only be cured by confession and rites of purification.[1]

An important place in African medicine is taken by amulets, designed to avert disease. These often resemble the fetiches used for the treatment of disease.

Several African people seem to possess in a definite form the idea of the causation of disease by climatic or other natural conditions, in which case their remedies may be purely medical and devoid of any religious character, though the nature of the remedies usually brings them nearer to those of the Middle Ages than of our own time. This development of a genuine art of medicine has been recorded among several Bantu peoples, but seems to have reached its greatest height among the Masai,[2] who are said never to ascribe disease to the action of spirits, and only rarely to human agency. We are told of only one disease, elephantiasis of the scrotum, which is regarded as a punishment for sin.

In addition to the modes of combating disease which are closely related to magic or religion, most African peoples employ remedies of a domestic kind which can be used by all, or measures employed by those who possess the necessary skill, but are yet quite distinct from the priests or wizards, who carry out rites which are magical or religious as well as medical. Among the remedies of this kind are blood-letting in the form of cupping, massage, various forms of surgery, and many internal remedies.

Among the Masai the internal remedies are known to all, and

---

[1] J. Roscoe, *op. cit.*, p. 102.
[2] M. Merker, *Die Masai*, Berlin, 1904, p. 174.

it is only surgical procedures which are practised by specialized practitioners. In some parts of Africa a man may have a reputation for success in the treatment of some one form of disease. As was found to be the case in Melanesia, where there has been specialization of medical function it has often proceeded along lines different from, and it may be even antagonistic to, those which would promote the separation of medicine from magic and religion.

AMERICA

This continent affords a good example of the intimate relation between medicine and religion, the combination having developed to such an extent that most of the religious rites, rites often very elaborate and prolonged, have as their main purpose the treatment of sickness.

The belief in the production of disease by human agency exists in North America, but it is less important and frequent than in many other parts of the world. When sickness is produced in this way, the agent is usually one who has many other functions in addition to those connected with disease.

Sickness is more usually ascribed to the action of ghosts or spirits, who act either on account of a natural malevolence, or because they have been offended by some lapse on the part of the victim, especially the breaking of a food taboo, or failure to follow the many observances connected with childbirth, puberty, menstruation, and coitus.

The most frequent belief concerning the mode of production of disease is to ascribe it to the introduction into the body of some noxious agent, which, though apparently primarily of a spiritual kind, is often objectified or personified. A frequent object thus regarded as the immediate cause of disease is a piece of bone, and as frequently an animal, either a worm or insect, or it may be an animal as large as a bear or otter. A less frequent belief concerning the causation of disease is that which we have met elsewhere, in which disease is ascribed to the absence of the soul or one of several souls. Disease may also be assigned to natural causes, such as the action of the moon or of the winds.

As elsewhere, the chief lines of treatment of disease in America are the logical outcome of the beliefs in causation. They consist of rites of exorcism, in which the disease possessing the patient is driven away by incantations, the noise of rattles and drums, and other means. In other cases the objectified disease is abstracted by sucking or other forms of legerdemain. When disease is ascribed to a loss of the soul, it is recovered by a leech; and it is sometimes believed that, as in Indonesia and Melanesia, the soul of a leech leaves his body in order to recover the lost soul of the patient. Disease may be transferred to an animal or to another person. In the highly developed rites of the medicine societies of the Pueblo Indian, the Navaho and Apache, all the members of the society assist in the rites designed to restore health to a sick person, who defrays the whole cost of the ceremonial.

In addition to these lines of treatment, which bring medicine into such close relations with religion, a number of measures, including plants as internal remedies, blood-letting, cauterization, poulticing, massage, and vapour baths, are employed.

The civilized peoples who inhabited Mexico and Central America when these countries were conquered by the Spaniards practised an art of medicine which bore a general resemblance to that of other parts of America, though of a more advanced kind.

Among the Aztecs, of whose medicine the record is most complete, the occurrence of disease was usually ascribed to the gods, though sorcery was occasionally held responsible. An illness was often believed to follow some fault on the part of the patient, usually some breach of ritual. There were special gods of disease. In Mexico they not only inflicted disease, but there were special deities of healing, one such being a goddess of herbs, and another one who had discovered the curative properties of turpentine.

Corresponding with this belief in the divine origin of disease, diagnosis and prognosis often took the form of divination, and the course of an illness was foretold by scrying in a mirror or in water, or by the unravelling of a knot. The remedies included an extensive pharmacopœia, in which plants predominated, while bleeding, vapour baths, and massage were widely employed. Rites of exorcism were also used, while among this advanced people we meet again the form of treatment in which the leech pretends to suck from the body of his patient a pebble or other object, which was held to have been implanted there by human or spiritual agency, and to have been the cause of the illness.

Disease was also transferred from one person to another. A figure of dough, made in human form, was placed by the roadside so that it might enter the next passer-by, a process bearing the closest resemblance to one I have already mentioned as occurring in West Africa.

The existing rude peoples of Central America practise similar methods. One tribe of the Mosquito Indians of Nicaragua has the peculiar custom that six persons are urged to eat as much as possible, especially of green turtle.

In many parts of South America the belief in human agency in the production of disease is especially prominent. Thus, in British Guiana, every disease is regarded as the work of a sorcerer, and an illness ascribed to his spells is treated by one of a class of practitioner, who pretends to extract an object placed in the body of the patient by the sorcerer.[1]

The Incas of Peru had an extensive pharmacopœia, and practised vinesection, but we do not know that their religious rites were as closely connected with health and disease as was the case

[1] E. im Thurn, *Among the Indians of Guiana*, London, 1883, pp. 329 *sqq.*

among the Aztecs and Mayas. The Mapuche of Chili[1] have two classes of priest, of which one also acted as leeches, while surgeons form still another body of specialized practitioners. Those who were at once leeches and priests are said to be concerned with spirits, to whose action it would seem that disease was attributed. The Mapuche use many herbs and employ venesection, massage, and vapour-baths.

SIMILARITY IN VIEWS ON CAUSATION AND TREATMENT OF DISEASE

This survey, brief though it be, is sufficient to show how great a similarity exists between different regions of the earth in the general character of the beliefs concerning the causation of disease, and in the measures which are used to combat its effects. As I have already said, these similarities have been held by most students of human society to be the result of uniformity in the working of the human mind in response to its environment. They are held to be examples of similarity in the course of evolution, owing to similarity of the materials which the process of evolution moulds and uniformity of the agency by which this moulding is carried out. Only when the similarities occur among neighbouring peoples, who though distant from one another, are known to have been in contact, has it been customary to explain them by the transmission of culture from one place to another. Otherwise they have been supposed to have arisen independently, and this view is still[2] widely held. Its advocates fail to see how in early stages of his culture man can have moved about the world with sufficient freedom to produce the wide dispersal of object and custom which must have occurred if these similarities are due to transmission. I propose

[1] O. Aichel, *Arch. f. Geschichte d. Medizin*, 1913, vi, p. 161.
[2] 1917.

to consider the rival views, according to which these similarities depend upon transmission, or are the result of processes of independent origin.

CONSIDERATION OF RIVAL VIEWS

I may first point out how favourable a case for independent origin is presented by the phenomena of disease. Many of the similarities of culture which are believed to have come into being independently in different parts of the world, relate to features of man's environment which are far from uniform. Thus, different parts of the earth show great differences in the apparent movements of the sun, and in the course and nature of the seasons. As great variations are shown in the nature and annual changes of vegetation, and in the natural features of land and sea. If the human mind is the same everywhere, these differences in the physical environment should lead us to expect diversity rather than uniformity in the customs relating to them. Where we find similarities of reaction towards the sun, the seasons, vegetation, and other natural conditions in places where Nature presents herself under such widely diverse aspects, the advocate of the independent origin of these similarities is met at the outset by a serious difficulty.[1]

[1] [A very curious method of controversy has recently been devised by certain ethnologists, more especially in America, to evade the logical consequences of their claim for uniformity of reaction. Without consciously abandoning the doctrine of independent development of custom and belief, they somewhat inconsequently accuse those of us who criticize their interpretation of the facts of exaggerating the resemblances, which with a singular lack of cogency they pretend are superficial and spurious. But they seem to forget that the theory of the similarity of the working of the human mind, of which those who make the protests are themselves the champions, is wholly based upon the assumption that the resemblances are real and fundamental! Within recent years both Dr. Clark Wissler (*The American Indian*) and D. S. G. Morley (*The Ruins of Copan*) have employed this strange method of attack in criticizing me.—G. E. S.]

This initial difficulty is not present, or is present in much less degree, where man himself is more directly concerned. The phenomena of birth and death are the same everywhere. The difficulty which here meets the believer in independent origin is to explain the great diversity which is shown by a man's mode of reaction towards the occurrences of his own life.

This similarity of conditions throughout the world is also presented, though in somewhat less degree, by the phenomena of disease. With our advanced knowledge we recognize a considerable degree of diversity in the diseases of different parts of the world, but, in his ruder phases of development, man deals with symptoms rather than with diseases, or, more strictly speaking, does so in even greater measure than ourselves. The chief manifestations of disease, pain, fever, disturbances of the digestion, swellings, ulcerations, and eruptions, are much the same everywhere, and present a body of appearances showing so great a natural similarity that disease offers a most favourable opportunity for the advocates of independent origin. If they fail to show that similarities in the reaction of mankind towards disease have been the result of independent discovery and invention, it is difficult to see where they are likely to succeed.

TWO WIDELY DIFFERING BELIEFS IN CAUSATION OF DISEASE

I can only consider briefly two problems suggested by the material laid before you in this book. These will serve to illustrate the kind of situation with which we are confronted in this subject.

The sketch I have given, of the beliefs and practices of different regions of the earth in relation to disease, has brought out certain differences in the distribution of the customs which bring medicine into intimate relations with magic and religion.

The belief in the production of disease by the abstraction of the soul, of some part of the soul, or of one of several souls, appears to be limited to Indonesia, Papuo-Melanesia, and America. We do not know of it in Asia; and, though disease may be ascribed to absence of the soul or of the vital principle in West Africa, this belief does not appear to have given rise to the organized system of practices which we find in Indonesia and, to a less extent, in America.

India and Africa, on the other hand, are pre-eminently the seat of the belief in the production of disease by possession. These two beliefs, one in the production of disease by the addition of something to the body of the patient, the other in the abstraction of something from it, are more or less opposed to one another.[1] If the phenomena of disease are much the same all the world over, and if the similarities of belief and action are due to the uniformity of the human mind, how comes it that men should have been led to these very different beliefs and why should these beliefs have different distributions?

The advocate of independent origin ought to be able to point to something in the nature of the diseases of Indonesia, or in their relation to the environment, which led the inhabitants of this region to attach so great an importance to the abstraction of the soul, while the peoples of India and Africa failed to make such a discovery, or, if they believed in the absence of the soul as a cause of illness, failed to make it the basis of their system of therapeutics.

Still more difficult is the task of explaining the co-existence of these widely different, if not opposed, beliefs among one people, as in North America. If, as the majority of students of American ethnography hold, the culture of this continent has

---

[1] These opposed beliefs may sometimes be brought into relation with one another. Thus the Ewe-speaking peoples of West Africa believe that when the soul of a person quits his body it provides an opportunity for a wandering, homeless spirit to enter and produce disease. A. B. Ellis, *The Ewe-speaking Peoples*, London, 1890, p. 107.

been the result of a wholly independent process of development, we should hardly expect to find two such widely different modes of conceiving the essential nature of disease. The co-existence of two such concepts is far more naturally explained as the result of the contact of peoples and the blending of their cultures.

This solution of the problem becomes still more natural when we find the belief in the production of disease by the abstraction of a soul especially frequent and important on the western side of the American continent—viz. in that part which forms one shore of an ocean, on the other side of which this belief flourishes. Very significant in this connexion is the condition found among the Songish, whose women are able to cure disease due to causes other than loss of the soul, while a lost soul can only be recovered by one of a special class of shamans.

REMEDIES OF THE "DOMESTIC" ORDER

The second problem which I choose for the purpose of illustration, is suggested by certain difference which distinguish the domestic remedies of many peoples from those which are, or should be, applied only by persons with especial qualifications. Earlier in this book I showed that the means of combating disease adopted by the peoples of Melanesia and New Guinea follow naturally from their beliefs concerning its causation. Once we know the Melanesian or Papuan theory of disease, their diagnostic and therapeutic measures are seen to be only the logical consequences of this theory. Actions which may seem meaningless or even ridiculous on superficial examination, are only the natural outcome of the views which the people hold concerning the nature of the disease. I stated, however, that there were exceptions. It is in the remedies which may be applied to anyone, and do not need the services of a specially qualified practitioner, that these exceptions are most apparent.

These remedies correspond very closely with those which among ourselves we call "domestic"—remedies used by anyone in cases of slight illness, or at the first onset of more serious illness before its gravity is recognized. Just as among ourselves, the doctor is only sent for when domestic remedies fail, or when the illness is at once seen to be serious, so do the Melanesian, Papuan, and other lowly peoples only consult the sorcerer, priest, or leech when their remedies of the domestic order fail, or when the gravity of the case demands more powerful measures.

The nature of these domestic remedies is well illustrated by the Kai, a people of North-Eastern New Guinea, of whose prolonged and complex ritual, based on the belief in abstraction of the soul or soul-substance, I have given so full an account (see pp. 84 seq.). In addition to the measures which involve the activity of the sorcerer or leech, the Kai use a number of remedies which seem to have no connexion with the concept of soul-substance. For wounds they use a rude kind of poultice made of the powdered fruits of the cycas-palm covered with its leaves, and various kinds of leaf or bark are believed to have a healing action upon wounds.

The abstraction of blood is an almost universal remedy. Freshly inflicted wounds are made to bleed as freely as possible, and unless this is done it is believed that the wound will never heal. It is held that the bad blood flows away, while the good blood remains in the body. Headache is treated by cuts on the forehead, made with splinters, formerly of obsidian and now of glass. In cases of nasal catarrh a stick is thrust into the nostrils to make them bleed, and this treatment is also used in cases of illness in which the nose is not itself affected. Blood is also drawn by leeches applied to parts of the body which are the seat of pain.

For pain in the chest with difficulty of breathing, the people stroke the chest with a kind of nettle, and this remedy is also used to get rid of the muscular pain which follows long marches or the bearing of very heavy loads. Vapour-baths, used for rheumatic pains, are produced by heated stones, lying on and covered by leaves, placed in a hole dug in the earth. The painful part of the body is exposed to the vapour which rises from the leaves, or steam may be produced by putting hot stones into the coconut vessels which are used to carry water. Kneading of the body is sometimes employed. A curious remedy is used for deafness due to occlusion of the external auditory meatus. A small chafer is introduced into the passage and may remain there for several days. This method of cleaning what Keysser calls the Augean stable of the Papuan ear is believed to be highly efficacious in the restoration of hearing.

This lowly people of New Guinea thus use more or less rude forms of five modes of treatment which are found widely over the earth—viz. poulticing, blood-letting, massage, vapour-baths, and counter-irritation. Moreover, these practices stand apart from the system of therapeutics based on the belief in the production of disease by human or spiritual agency, which bulks so largely in the minds of the people.

It would be easy to point out ways in which each one of the measures found among the Kai might have been discovered by the process called chance or accident. The whole history of invention shows, however, that new discoveries do not arise in this way, but are the direct outcome of the physical and social conditions in which they have their birth. Even if inventions come to fruition by mere accident, it would still be difficult to accept the position that these rude savages discovered, independently and by chance, five of the procedures of our own mediaeval and modern medicine.

If we are to explain the independent origin of these Papuan practices, we ought to be able to show that they arose out of the body of beliefs concerning the causation of disease, and this is just what we cannot do. The Kai have a definite body of beliefs concerning the causation of disease, to which corresponds a definite system of therapeutics, but this system does not include the remedies I have just enumerated, nor does it seem possible to show that these remedies are in any way connected with the dominant beliefs concerning the causation of disease.

ORIGIN OF ABOVE PRACTICES

The survey of the medicine of other parts of the world which I have given in this chapter shows that what is true of the Kai is true of nearly all the more lowly peoples of the earth. When we find such peoples practising venesection and cupping, and using massage and vapour-baths, etc., these practices do not form part of the blend of religion and medicine which is the most striking characteristic of the attitude of these peoples towards disease. They are not practised by the special class of persons who combine in various degrees the functions of the priest and leech, but they may be performed by anyone, or by persons who have acquired a special reputation for skill in these respects by practice and ability, not through the special processes of initiation which are usually necessary for the practice of the rites in which medicine and religion are so closely blended. In many cases even these forms of treatment are exercised by women, who are so often rigorously excluded from participation in medico-religious rites.

Most of the peoples of the earth who use blood-letting, massage, and vapour-baths, have certainly not been led to these practices by motives arising out of the ideas and beliefs regarding disease which dominate the larger part of their behaviour in the presence of disease. If they have arisen independently in different parts of the earth, they have not grown out of the magico-religious atmosphere which surrounds disease. They must rather be ascribed to some kind of reaction against this religious atmosphere, to a movement on the part of the general body of the people against a view of disease forming part of a system of beliefs which regulate behaviour, not only towards disease, but towards many other aspects of nature. The special arguments against independent origin, which each of the customs suggests when examined independently, are strongly reinforced by the absence of any relation to the body of beliefs which determine the attitude of the more lowly peoples of the earth towards disease.

It is, of course, open to the advocates of independent origin to say that such practices as blood-letting and vapour-baths, as they exist in New Guinea, are only the beginnings of a movement towards rational medicine among a people who had till then been altogether dominated by a system of sorcery or priestcraft. They may say that the rude forms in which these remedies occur are natural as the first product of trends of thought which have produced the more elaborate and finished forms of these practices among ourselves. In response to such an argument I will now make only one suggestion.

Highly as we rate our own civilization, it did not enable us to discover for ourselves practices which, according to advocates of independent origin, must have been discovered by the Melanesian and Papuan. We acquired our practices of bleeding and counter-irritation from the Greeks or Arabs, our massage from the French or other continental people, and our vapour-baths from the Turks and Russians. The civilization of which we are so proud did not of itself suffice to teach us these remedial arts, but we had to acquire them by contact and mixture with other peoples. If we are to accept the teachings of those who believe in the independent origin of such practices in Africa, Asia, Oceania, and America, we shall have to accept the position that the savage or barbarous peoples who inhabit these continents and islands were somehow able to discover arts which we, who think ourselves so greatly their superiors, were content to learn from other peoples.

4

In the last chapter I gave some account of the present condition of the science of ethnology in its bearing on the problems raised by the complex relations between medicine, magic, and religion. It was seen that there is a great similarity throughout the world, not only in those practices which bring medicine into intimate relations with magic and religion, but also in the domestic or strictly medical remedies so often found side by side with those used by the magician and the priest. The problem now in special need of solution is whether these similar practices have arisen independently in different parts of the earth, or have developed in some one locality, whence they have been carried to their present areas of distribution by the wanderings of people.

In the last chapter I illustrated certain difficulties which meet us when we attempt the explanation of these similarities on the hypothesis of independent origin. The co-existence of two more or less opposed beliefs concerning the causation of disease in America, and the failure to derive the domestic remedies of a lowly Papuan people from their theory of disease, are difficult to explain on this hypothesis, while they are easy to understand if the movements of mankind over the earth's surface in early times were more extensive than has hitherto been supposed.

It is one thing, however, to state a case for transmission. It is another thing to demonstrate its importance in the history of human culture. The case for this mode of explaining the similarities of human culture will only be complete when we are able to point to certain regions of the earth as the places of origin of similar practices, and when we have discovered by whom the practices were carried over the earth and the course taken by these travellers. I propose to begin to-day with a brief consideration of the methods by which the science of ethnology is now seeking the solution of such problems as those suggested by the facts laid before you in the last chapter.

METHODS OF SOLVING THE PROBLEMS

In considering the methods by which we may hope to attain a knowledge of the manifold changes which have taken place in the relations between medicine, magic, and religion during the history of mankind, the first point to be noted is that we cannot expect to succeed if we limit our attention entirely to the special subject we are hoping to elucidate. The social life of man is so complex, the various elements of which it is built up form so closely interwoven a structure, especially in the lowly examples of culture with which we are now dealing, that we cannot expect to understand a part except in its relation to the whole.

THE IMPORTANCE ATTACHED TO NUMBERS

I may illustrate this subject by considering for a moment a feature of medical practice in which numbers are concerned. It is the custom of certain peoples that a therapeutic measure shall be repeated a definite number of times—three, four, five, or seven, as the case may be. A striking example from Eddystone Island, in the Solomons, was given in Chapter 2 (see p. 31). In this island, a treatment usually lasts for four days, sometimes for four days in each of four successive months.

This importance of the number four in medical practice is far from unique. The ancient Egyptians also had a four-day cure, and among the Cherokee of North America the normal length of a course of treatment is four days.[1]

Whether this striking agreement between ancient Egypt, the Solomon Islands, and North America is the result of the spread of culture, or whether the period of four days has been independently chosen in the three widely separated localities, is not a problem which can be settled by the study of medicine alone. Both in Eddystone Island and North America the fourfold nature of the medical rites forms only part of a system which makes the number four of the greatest importance throughout the whole range of ceremonial, whether medical, magical, or religious. In both places the four-day cure is only one manifestation of a belief which ascribes special virtue to the number four.

A wider survey shows that, though we do not know of a four-day cure in Indonesia, the number is of great importance not only in religious ceremonial but also in connexion with disease. Thus, when a patient is isolated with an *adu* in front of him in the island of Nias, the isolation lasts for four days. Again, in the proceeding of initiation by which a youth is fitted for the duties of a priest, his instruction in the proper use of the gong and in the appropriate formulas lasts for four days. In a different department of custom, food is put aside for the use of the ghost for four days after death, and for these four days the people do not go into the rice-fields. Again, in countries so widely separated as Greece and Japan, we find a four-fold classification prominent. For Greece, I need only refer to the four elements, the four humours, etc. The question whether the existence of a four-day

---

[1] J. Mooney, *Journ. Amer. Folk-lore*, 1890, iii, 48.

cure in Egypt, Eddystone Island, and North America is due to transmission or to independent origin is only part of the much larger question whether Egypt, Greece, Indonesia, Japan, the Solomon Islands, and North America possess geographical, climatic, or other feature in common which have led their inhabitants to attach particular importance to the number four, or whether this number acquired in some one part of the world a religious importance with which it passed elsewhere as a constituent element of a migrant culture.[1]

THE CRITERION OF COMMON DISTRIBUTION

This need for a broad and comprehensive study becomes especially apparent in the chief method by which the ethnologist is now striving to build up schemes of the history of human institutions. For this purpose one of his chief instruments is the criterion of common distribution. If we map out the distribution over the earth of two customs between which no natural relationship can be discovered, and find that the areas of distribution correspond, and if this correspondence of distribution cannot be traced to any uniform climatic or other geographical conditions, we conclude that the association between the two customs came into existence in some part of the earth, and was spread thence by the movements of people, either in the course of definite migrations or for the purpose of trade.[2]

Thus no natural connexion can be found between the worship of the sun and the practice of building megalithic monuments. When, therefore, we find these two customs associated together in some parts of the world, while both are absent in others, the

---

[1] [It was not until August, 1918, in the year following the delivery of these lectures, that Dr. Rivers admitted the Egyptian origin of civilization—after three years of discussion and critical examination of the evidence.]

[2] [Exploitation is perhaps the more appropriate word.]

chances against their independent origin become very much greater than if no such agreement of distribution existed. When instead of two such associated customs we find many, the chances against their independent origin become very great.

SOME DIFFICULTIES MET WITH

We are at present only on the threshold of the quest by which we may hope to break up the complex web of human culture into its component strands, by which we may assign each element of culture to a definite movement of mankind. Our immediate task is to show the principles to be employed in this quest, and the methods by which these principles may be applied. I propose to devote the chief part of this chapter to certain difficulties which meet us when we use the criterion of common distribution as our test for transmission.

If a culture has been transported over the earth from a locality in which it has developed, we must expect to find gaps in the chain of evidence. We must expect that one element of culture will fail to implant itself here and another there; that other elements will be modified in their new home, sometimes, perhaps to such an extent as to make it difficult to recognize the relation of the final product to the custom in which it had its source. I will begin by formulating a principle which may guide us in our inquiry into such cases of disappearance and modification. I shall then inquire whether it is possible to see the working of this principle when we study the nature and distribution of a small group of therapeutic and hygienic customs.

I have already suggested that a medical practice in a new home may lose its therapeutic character and become part of a indigenous magical or religious cult. On the other hand, an introduced magical or religious practice may receive a therapeutic application which it did not possess in its original home.

FORMULATION OF GUIDING PRINCIPLE

The kind of process which ensues when a culture is transplanted into a new home may be formulated as follows. Transplanted elements of culture tend to take root in a new home in so far as they are in harmony with the physical and cultural nature of their new environment, and, if they succeed in taking root, tend to become modified in the direction of the indigenous culture by which they are assimilated. This proposition has two parts— one dealing with the success or failure of new elements of culture to survive in a new home; the other, with the tendency to modification which shows itself in greater or less degree in cases of success.

FACTORS AFFECTING SUCCESS OR FAILURE OF TRANSPLANTED ELEMENTS OF CULTURE

Physical conditions are often such as to prevent the introduction of customs which would otherwise form part of a culture-complex. Thus, the absence of suitable earth may lead to a disappearance of pottery, or the difficulty of obtaining stone may lead to the degeneration of megalithic monuments, so that they resemble those of other parts of the world in form only and not in size.

Less obvious, but quite as important, are characters of the social environment into which a new element of culture is conveyed. This environment may be so adverse to the newly introduced practice that, if this succeeds in implanting itself at all, it soon withers and disappears under the opposition of indigenous trends of thought and action. Thus, it is probably the very different nature of the social environment of Melanesia and Polynesia which has led to a remarkable difference between these two regions in respect to their use of strictly medical practices. Medical and surgical remedies comparable with those of civilized peoples are of more frequent occurrence in Melanesia than in Polynesia. Even when strictly medical or surgical practices are found in Polynesia, there is often evidence that they have only recently been introduced. This difference between the two ethnographic provinces presents us with a striking problem which seems at first sight difficult to explain, either on the hypothesis of transmission, or on that of independent origin. The Polynesians are undoubtedly more intelligent people than the Melanesians, and, if we take our own civilization as the standard, Polynesian culture has reached a considerably higher level of development than that of Melanesia. If we believe that any medical and surgical remedies have been discovered independently in this part of the world, it is difficult to understand why the more intelligent and cultivated people should have fallen behind in these discoveries.

If, on the other hand, we look at the matter from the point of view furnished by the hypothesis of transmission, we meet a problem of great interest. If this hypothesis is to work we shall have to find some reason why medical and surgical practices have been adopted by the lowly Melanesian in fuller measure than by the cultured Polynesian. I suggest that the reason becomes apparent if we apply the principle which I have just enunciated.

We have seen that the special characteristic of the Polynesian is the highly religious nature of his life. Disease is ascribed wholly to the action of gods and other spiritual beings, and its cure is mainly, in some cases entirely, sought by means of appeal to these higher powers. In Melanesia, on the other hand, disease is ascribed either to direct human agency, or to spiritual agency which is more or less under human guidance or control. The measures employed to remedy the action of spiritual beings involve the intervention of persons whose knowledge and power are believed to be essential to success.

Let us now try to imagine the nature of the process which

would follow the introduction of a medical or surgical practice among each people. There can be little question which would give it the heartier reception, which culture would be endowed with beliefs and sentiments to form the more appropriate soil for the growth of the new custom.

However closely a system of medicine be founded upon the belief in the working of a natural law, there can be no question that, in fact, and still more in the minds of both practitioner and patient, success depends upon individual skill and on the human factor. If this be so among ourselves, how much more must it be true of medical and surgical remedies introduced by strangers among a people who know nothing of natural law as we understand it? Such people will inevitably ascribe any success which follows the application of the remedy to the power of the man who has brought it among them, and by whom it is applied. The human factor will bulk so largely in their estimate of the value of the new remedy that its use will at once fall into line with those indigenous practices which involve the idea of human agency. To a people, on the other hand, imbued with the belief in the agency of higher powers, such remedies will not appeal. They may even be regarded as sacrilegious attempts to struggle against the will of the gods.

If, when certain medical remedies were introduced into Oceania, the differences between Melanesian and Polynesian were what they are to-day, or even if they were of the same general order, we are furnished with an explanation of the greater prevalence of strictly medical practices among the more lowly people. This example suggests how the presence or absence of an introduced medical practice may be determined by the nature of the indigenous culture into which it is received, by the degree in which it is adapted to the beliefs and sentiments natural to the people.

An example of a different kind is given in the distribution of blood-letting in the East. This practice, in the form of venesection, cupping, and leeching, is well established in India, but is almost completely absent in China, although several of the medical arts of this country are known to have come from India. Those who have recorded the absence or rarity of blood-letting in China note that it is due to the dislike of the spilling of blood which is characteristic of its people, a dislike which is chiefly responsible for the low state of Chinese surgery. That the practice of blood-letting is not indigenous in China is rendered highly probable by the existence of the dry method of cupping. If we believe that this practice has been developed independently in China, we shall be driven into the position that a people, who so objected to the sight of blood that the almost universal practice of blood-letting is hardly known among them, were nevertheless led to discover a high specialized therapeutic measure which elsewhere is intimately associated with blood-letting.

Still another indication that the knowledge of blood-letting reached China is shown by the fact that leeches are used for a medical purpose. They are sometimes applied to the cervix uteri in order to induce abortion.

The absence or rarity of blood-letting, combined with the process of dry-cupping and the medicinal use of leeches, receive as natural explanation if the various forms of blood-letting known in India were transported to China, but met with a poor reception, owing to their being in conflict with the beliefs and sentiments of the Chinese in connexion with blood, while the practice of dry-cupping, which does not involve the spilling of blood, became an important part of their therapeutic practice.

MODIFICATION OF PRACTICES
AFTER INTRODUCTION

I can now turn to the second part of my subject, the modification of introduced practices due to the influence of the environment, physical and social, to which they are exposed. I may begin by considering a few examples of this process of modification taken from other departments of social life.

The modification of introduced practices occurs through the whole range of human culture. Whenever an element of culture, whether it be a word, a grammatical form, a religious practice, a social custom, or a material object, passes from one part of the world to another, it tends to become changed in the process, it does not remain in its new home what it was in its old.

In the domain of language, the process is so obvious that comment is hardly needed, especially to us whose speech is full of words taken from languages widely different from its original Anglo-Saxon basis. I may refer, however, for a moment to the words with which the English language is now being enriched as a consequence of the war. The new French and German words which are finding their way into our speech not only differ from the original in grammatical form, and still more in pronunciation, but they are acquiring special meanings, and in some cases have already assumed a form which would make it difficult for the most expert philologists to trace their origin. The derivation of the "napoo" of the British soldier from the "il n'y a plus" is a good example.

Another striking example of modification occurs in the case of decorative art. A mode of artistic expression introduced into a new home never remains the same. The art of a country resembles every other product of human society in becoming conventionalized and subject to definite laws or canons. No new form of art can escape the influence of these conventions. Thus, an introduced human motive may be changed as the result of its assimilation by a conventionalized geometrical art, so that no one would recognize the human form in the final product, if it were not for intermediate forms which give the clue to its origin and development.[1]

[1] W. H. R. Rivers, *Rep. Brit. Assoc.*, Dundee, 1912, p. 599; *History of Melanesian Society*, Cambridge, 1914, ii, p. 374.

The laws governing the modification of introduced elements of culture, which I have illustrated by examples taken from language and art, apply also to the practices and beliefs which make up the art of medicine. If medical and surgical practices have been transmitted from one part of the world to another we must not expect exact resemblances. Not only must we look for modifications, developments, and simplifications, but we must also be prepared for changes so great that, without intermediate stages in the process of transformation, it would be impossible to recognize a practice, perhaps no longer therapeutic at all, into which an introduced medical practice has been transformed.

EXAMPLES SUGGESTED AS MODIFICATIONS OF TRANSMITTED PRACTICES

I shall now consider some examples in which practices, the transportation of which from one part of the earth to another I shall assume, seem to have suffered change. As I have already said, the scientific demonstration of such change can only be a gradual process resting upon a far wider study than is possible on such an occasion as this. My object to-day is rather to suggest certain medical and surgical processes as fit subjects for this line of study.

BLOOD-LETTING

I will begin with a possibility suggested by the Chinese attitude towards blood-letting, which I dealt with just now. We saw that though the letting of blood is rarely practised in China, the closely allied practice of dry-cupping is taking a prominent place in the medical practice of its people. The possibility is suggested that this practice arose in China as the result of the modification of wet-cupping, as a result of the objection of the Chinese to the shedding of blood. Whether this be so, or whether dry-cupping is the only survivor of a group of introduced practices, is a question which can only be answered on the basis of a wider survey than is possible here (I may say now that this survey will almost certainly show that the practice of dry-cupping did not arise in China).

Another case in which the practice of blood-letting may have suffered modification, in aim if not in method, is suggested by the frequency of blood-letting as a religious rite. In many parts of the world the letting of blood by means of incisions or scarifications forms part of a religious ritual, while in other cases it is a feature of the customs accompanying mourning for the dead, and other social practices, which probably have or have had a religious significance. The problem arises whether there is any relation between this form of blood-letting and that which has a therapeutic purpose. We know of a few facts which point to a connexion between the two kinds of practice. Thus, in Polynesia the letting of blood by means of gashes and scarifications as a therapeutic practice is specially characteristic of the western islands, such as Samoa, and seems to be in vogue to a much smaller extent in the Eastern Pacific. A similar difference characterizes the two regions in regard to the letting of blood for religious purposes, of which we hear far more in the Western than in the Eastern Pacific. The common distribution of the therapeutic and religious forms of blood-letting in the Pacific suggests that there is a definite connexion between the two. It is possible that we have here a case in which a medical practice, introduced into the highly religious atmosphere of Polynesia, has come to form part of religious ceremonial and ordinary social custom, while still continuing to be used therapeutically.

MASSAGE

The modification of a medical practice when introduced into a new environment would seem to be well illustrated by massage.

I have elsewhere[1] drawn attention to this possibility. The natives of Eddystone Island in the Solomons employ manipulations which so closely resemble those of our own massage that, if simply observed, and not made the subject of special inquiry, they would undoubtedly be regarded as the equivalent of this remedy as practised by ourselves. Inquiry showed, however, that the object of the manipulations of the Eddystone leech in one case was to act upon an imaginary octopus, which was supposed to have taken up its abode in the body of a patient, while in other cases the object was to extract from the body an immaterial object or principle, which was held to be the cause of fever or other form of disease.

That the manipulations of the Solomon Islands stand in a definite relation to massage is rendered highly probable by the occurrence of genuine massage among the Polynesians, a people with whose culture that of Melanesia has much in common. Thus, in Samoa[2] two forms of massage are practised, each with a special name. That called milimili consists of gentle rubbing with the finger-tips, while the other, lomilomi, takes the form of kneading movements similar to those of our own practice. Both are used to remove pain, and as a restorative in cases of fatigue.

In the Tonga Islands three different operations are recognized.[3] One called mili consists of rubbing movements; another, fota, takes the form of compression; while in the third, called tugitugi, the body is beaten. Massage is widely used in other parts of Polynesia. Sometimes it assumes peculiar forms. Thus, in the Hawaiian Islands, heavy objects are rolled along the body; in the Tongan Islands a man who is fatigued will get three or four

---

[1] Proc. Internat. *Congress of Medicine*, London, 1913, section xxiii, p. 139; reprinted in *Psychology and Ethnology*, London, 1926, p. 57.

[2] J. B. Stair, *Old Samoa*, 1897, p. 165.

[3] Mariner, *Tonga*, London, 1817, ii, 350.

children to trample him all over; and a similar method is used in the Eastern Pacific.

Massage is widely employed in America, and is very prominent in the therapeutic system of China and Japan. In Japan the practice is said to go back to the time of the Emperor Jimmu (660–585 B.C.). The blind are employed as masseurs, and the movements they use include rubbing, kneading, pressing, and striking, according to definite rules. Chamberlain[1] records a feature of Japanese massage which is of distinct interest in relation to the point which I am now considering. He notes that formerly the Japanese always massaged the limbs downwards, and have only adopted the practice of rubbing towards the trunk from Europeans. This downward direction of movements is characteristic of Melanesia and other places, where it is intended to expel injurious agencies from the body, the object being to force or induce the spirit inhabiting the limb to quit it at the extremity.

There is no question that the massage of Japan is a practice as definitely therapeutic as among ourselves, but the centrifugal direction of its manipulations suggests a relation to the belief in the causation of disease by objects or beings which it is the object of the massage to expel.

These examples are, I think, sufficient to show that there is a connexion between the therapeutic and hygienic art of massage and the manipulations by which many peoples extract or expel from the body agencies, material, or immaterial, which they believe to be the causes of disease. I must be content now to raise the problem, and leave for a survey on a far wider basis the consideration whether the latter usage has arisen through modification of an introduced therapeutic practice, or whether the therapeutic use has grown out of an older practice, resting upon magical or religious beliefs. I will only say here that in Oceania there is little doubt about the answer. The highly developed

[1] *Things Japanese*, London, 1905, p. 316.

massage of Polynesia has almost certainly been introduced into Melanesia either by the Polynesians themselves, or more probably by the immigrant people who form the upper stratum of Polynesian society. If so introduced, it has certainly been modified in accordance with the indigenous ideas of the Melanesian concerning the causation and nature of disease.

SWEAT-BATHS

In the case of massage I have been dealing with the relation between a practice so definitely therapeutic that it forms part of our own system of medicine and a group of practices which, while still related to disease, yet bear the stamp of magic or charlatanry rather than of genuine medicine. A problem of a different kind presents itself in the use of vapour-baths, which, in one form or another, have a very wide distribution among the peoples of the earth.

The practice of exposing the body, or some part of it, to heat so as to produce sweating is found in a more or less crude form in Melanesia, New Guinea, Polynesia, Africa, and America, as well as in the eastern countries from which we have ourselves largely or altogether derived the practice. (The sweat-houses of Ireland suggest that the practice is ancient in Northern Europe, and that the modern Russian and Turkish forms are only improved forms of an old and indigenous Celtic or Teutonic practice.) Thus, in Melanesia, an injured limb will be exposed to the vapour rising from damp leaves or moss placed over a fire. In the Hawaiian Islands[1] the patient is enclosed in a hut within which steam is produced, and a similar practice occurs in Africa where, for instance, the Ba-Ronga[2] enclose a sick man in a small hut made of mats, and, by putting a pot with live embers by his side, cause him to sweat profusely.

[1] David Malo, *Hawaiian Antiquities*, Honolulu, 1903, p. 146.
[2] H. A. Junod, *Life of a South African Tribe*, Neuchatel, 1913, ii, 426.

The country in which the vapour-bath has reached its highest pitch of development is America, where, especially on the west coast, among the advanced Pueblo Indians of New Mexico and Arizona, and among the ancient Aztecs of Mexico, the sweat-house is a most important social institution. Among many North American peoples it was the representative of the men's club-house of Melanesia, and other parts of the world, which it resembled in the feature that women were rigorously excluded from its precincts. Among the Pueblo Indians the sweat-house has been described[1] as at once the bath-room, town-hall, council chamber, club-room, and church of the people.

If there is anything in common to the sweat-house of America and the vapour-baths of other parts of the world, it is evident that a process of modification must have taken place. If so, there can be little doubt that this process has been one in which a therapeutic and hygienic practice introduced into America has undergone a process of development, probably through a process of fusion with other social practices, whereby it has become one of the most important social institutions of the people.

CIRCUMCISION AND SUB-INCISION

A striking example of modification of an introduced practice is provided by circumcision among ourselves. At the present time this operation is performed in this country for two wholly different purposes. Among one section of the population it is a religious rite, intimately bound up with the social traditions of those who practise it, while among the general body of the people it is a hygienic practice still in process of development, and gradually coming more and more into vogue on account of its practical value.

There is no doubt that the great increase in the frequency of

---

[1] H. H. Bancroft, *Native Races of the Pacific States*, London, 1875, i, p. 537.

circumcision in this country is due to Jewish influence. The observation of the beneficial hygienic effects of the operation among the Jewish section of the population has made an operation, which formerly only entered into our system of surgery in cases of special need, one which is performed in childhood on a large section of the population. We have here a clear example in which an introduced religious practice has had a definite effect in fostering, if not in producing, a measure of hygienic surgery.

There is reason to suppose that one of the most extraordinary mutilations known to be practised by mankind is an example of a change in the opposite direction, an introduced surgical procedure having become a religious or magico-religious rite. The aborigines of Australia practise on their youth a mutilation, formerly known as the "terrible rite" and now as sub-incision, in which the urethra is opened to a great part of its length, sometimes from the perineum to the meatus. It is generally supposed that this operation is limited to Australia, and since this continent is usually regarded as one of the strongholds of the advocates of independent origin, ethnologists have been content to regard sub-incision as a wholly independent invention of the Australian aboriginal, an extension of the idea of mutilation of the genital organs, of which circumcision is the most frequent and widespread example.

A very similar operation, however, is practised in Fiji and Tonga, where it has a purely therapeutic purpose. Although the practice was originally Fijiian, our most complete description of it comes from Tonga.[1] The urethra is opened and a thread passed, so that one end hangs from the artificial opening and the other from the meatus. The thread acts as a seton, and is occasionally drawn backwards and forwards so as to produce pain and the discharge of blood. The operation is a favourite remedy for tetanus, and Mariner saw several cases in which its

[1] Mariner, *Tonga*, 1817, ii.

employment was followed by recovery. The operation is also employed in cases of injury accompanied, or believed to be accompanied, by extravasation of blood into the abdominal cavity, the motive being to get rid of the blood by way of the urethra.

The close resemblance between the Australian and the Fijiian practices suggests that they are related to one another. To suppose that two peoples, not very remote from one another geographically and resembling one another to some extent physically, were led to devise this extraordinary operation in total independence of one another, makes too great a demand on scientific credulity. We can be confident that the practice has been transmitted from one people to the other, or more probably, that the Australian and Fijiian practices are two different manifestations of a custom belonging to a migrant people who reached both localities. Here, as in the cases already considered, the evidence is not sufficient to show the primary purpose of the operation. It seems most likely that we have here an example of a surgical remedy which, introduced into Australia among a people greatly interested in mutilation as a feature of the ceremonial of initiation into manhood, was adopted and applied to this new purpose.

This subject has been considered in greater detail in my book *Psychology and Ethnology* (1926), p. 62.

SOME POINTS RAISED IN RELATION TO DISTRIBUTION OF CUSTOMS

If the hypothesis of transmission holds good, certain practices would seem to have been modified in the process of introduction among peoples with beliefs and customs widely different from those of the locality where the particular practices had their source. My aim has been to show that, in any attempt to work out the distribution of medical practices, we must study not merely the obviously diagnostic and therapeutic measures, but must also look for other manifestations, sometimes in a guise strangely different from that of the original custom.

It will not be possible to consider how far we can now construct a scheme in which the practices I have to-day considered can be assigned to definite movements of mankind over the earth's surface. In the scheme of migration put forward by Professor Elliot Smith[1] to account for the common distribution of megaliths, mummification, sun-cult, and other elements of culture, one of the customs I have considered to-day is included. The distribution of massage has suggested to Elliot Smith that this practice was carried over the earth by a people who mummified their dead, worshipped the sun, and constructed dolmens and other rude monuments of stone. It will not be possible here to consider this aspect of the subject fully; I must be content to point to a few facts which must be taken into account in such inquiries.

The distribution of the practice of blood-letting in Polynesia suggests that it belongs to a relatively late influence. It is especially prominent, both in religious rites and therapeutic practice, in the Samoan and Tongan Islands of the Western Pacific, where there is reason to suspect the relatively late influence of a people who, instead of exposing their dead on platforms, interred them in stone vaults in the extended position. In Melanesia we know of the practice of blood-letting in places where the influence of the people who interred their dead in the extended position is especially prominent. The distribution of blood-letting in Oceania suggests that it belongs to the relatively late influence of a people who interred their dead. The therapeutic practice of blood-letting is very prominent in India, and there is reason to believe that it is by the movements of a people who, while influencing India, were themselves largely influenced by its

<hr/>

[1] *The Migrations of Early Culture*, Manchester, 1915.

culture, that the practice of blood-letting has been spread over the earth.

The practice of massage, on the other hand, occurs throughout the Pacific, and is especially prominent in the eastern islands, such as Tahiti, where the dead are mummified on platforms or in canoes. The Polynesian distribution suggests the association of massage with a movement earlier than that which carried the practice of blood-letting.

Another point suggested by the distribution of customs which I have considered briefly in this chapter, is that sweatbaths and massage have travelled over the earth in company; just as they are closely associated among ourselves, so do they seem to be associated among many other peoples, suggesting that their diffusion was due to one and the same influence.

There are many other points which I should have liked to raise if there had been time. I can only refer here to the highly specialized character of such processes as venesection and cupping, which make it most unlikely that they have been discovered independently by the rude peoples who now practise them. I may also mention the frequent association throughout the world of the use of the cold plunge after the sweat-bath—a custom so little natural that its practice in Polynesia greatly excited the apprehensions of the early missionaries, who were evidently ignorant that a cold plunge was a feature of the sweat-bath of their own culture.

SCANTINESS OF AVAILABLE EVIDENCE

I have now considered a number of practices found in different parts of the world, with the object of seeing how they bear scrutiny under the two hypotheses of independent origin and transmission. I hope to have succeeded in showing that the hypothesis of independent origin furnishes a very inadequate explanation of the wide distribution of these practices, and often leads us into positions wholly at variance with the primary assumptions upon which the hypothesis rests. I have not been able to bring forward any absolutely conclusive evidence in favour of transmission, nor, when transmission seems probable, have I been able to point decisively to any one movement of mankind as its vehicle. As I have already stated, this is partly due to the fact that the demonstration of transmission must be reached by an argument in which each element of culture is studied in its relation to others, so that it only becomes possible through a far more comprehensive study than is possible on such an occasion as this. My object has been rather to suggest problems and consider the principles which we must follow in attempting their solution.

One fact which makes it impossible at present to reach any positive conclusion on these topics is the scantiness of the available evidence. There are few branches of human culture about which we know so little as in the case of medicine. Owing to the intimate relations between medicine, magic, and religion, much is to be learnt about the reaction of man towards disease from a study of the many researches on magic and religion which the wide interest in these subjects has produced. If the many medical men whose work takes them among peoples of lowly culture would take as much interest in the study of the ruder phases of their art as is taken by the missionary in the study of the religions he is trying to displace, we should soon be provided with a rich mass of ore from which to extract material for the construction of a history of the earlier phases of the practice of medicine.

HISTORY AND EVOLUTION

At the beginning of this book I distinguished between the historical and the so-called "evolutionary" treatment of the subject. It is with the historical aspect that I have so far chiefly dealt, with the ways in which the course of the history of medicine has been influenced by the movements of man and his culture over the earth's surface. We have seen that this course has not been one of simple progress, such as was once supposed to be characteristic of evolution. On the contrary, there has been revealed a complicated process of transformation in which it seems as if therapeutic measures of a more or less advanced kind, measures perhaps founded upon a rational pathology, have been transformed into religious or magical rites, or into social practices which have passed from generation to generation through the conservatism of mankind. The history of medicine, as illustrated by the ruder forms of human culture, seems to show a course in which degeneration has played as great a part as progress.

It must be noted that, when I speak of degeneration as shown by the transformation of medical practices into magical or religious rites, this is true only in so far as their medical character is concerned. We can only regard in this light a transformation by which a medical practice has wholly lost its therapeutic character. Few will object when we regard the transformation of a medical practice into a magical rite as an example of degeneration, but when we are dealing with transitions in the direction of religion it is necessary to bear in mind that the transformed medical practice may fulfil as high a social purpose as it fulfilled in its original character.

The frequency with which we seem to have found degeneration is largely due to the special character of this study, to its special occupation with the more backward peoples of the earth, peoples among whom we might expect to find degeneration bulking more largely than it would do in a wider survey of human society. As I have already said, we are only now emerging from a period in the study of human society during which the factor of degeneration has been almost wholly neglected or greatly underrated, even in the case of the ruder phases of human culture. In seeking to show how great a part degeneration has played, and is still playing, in the history of human society, we must be careful not to go to the opposite extreme, and overrate its frequency and importance.

COMPLEX NATURE OF THE PROCESS

If we survey the history of the practices which make up man's behaviour towards disease, there can be no question that, running through the complex web of change which this history shows, there has been a constant thread of progress. The degenerations and transformations shown so frequently in the history of medicine have only served to complicate a process in which man has succeeded more and more in bringing disease under control, in reducing the frequency and severity of pain, in remedying the many disabilities resulting from disease, and in rendering life longer and more secure.

This course has been complicated by two factors which have run counter to this progress. The growth of civilization has brought with it new forms of disease, or has increased the frequency of the old, chiefly as a result of inadequate adjustments of social means to the increasing complexity of social life. Thus, hardly an occupation has been developed by civilization which has not brought with it some new form, or has increased the liabilities to some old form, of disease. Perhaps still more important has been the increased tendency to instability of the mental life, due to the greater strain and stress to which advancing civilization exposes mankind. While man has been slowly forging weapons with which to combat disease, other lines of social progress have been producing new morbid states, to combat which these and still other weapons are required.

Again, the movements of mankind over the earth's surface, which have been one of the chief instruments in the progress of medicine, as of human culture in general, have themselves been the means by which mankind has distributed disease. In some cases the seeds of disease thus distributed have been the chief factors in the degeneration of culture, and in the disappearance of peoples who were the bearers of a culture from which perhaps our own advanced civilization might have much to learn. These ways, in which advancing culture has increased the opportunities for the onslaughts of disease, and has distributed its seeds, only serve, however, to complicate and obscure a process which is very real. Those who object to the crude evolutionary hypotheses of the last century do so, not because they believe the hypotheses of evolution to be false, but because their advocates have treated as simple a process which has been exceedingly complex. The opposition which is now showing itself more and more as this century progresses is not so much to evolution as to the evolutionist.

THE INFLUENCE OF CULTURAL MIXTURE ON PROGRESS

Not only have these discussions led us frequently to the process of degeneration, but this degeneration seems to have been especially the result of the contact of peoples and the blending of their cultures. Here again, however, the frequency with which we have found degeneration as the outcome of this contact and blending is due to the special limitations of the scope of this book. If we extend our survey we find that the history of medicine resembles that of every other branch of social life, in showing us an abundance of cases in which the movements of peoples and of their cultures have promoted progress. This is nowhere better illustrated than in the history of the movements whereby the cultures of India, Mesopotamia, Egypt, and Greece were brought into contact, producing a great wave of progress which overflowed to Italy and Spain, and through these channels came to have so great an influence on the medical art of our forefathers.

This influence of cultural mixture upon the course of progress has now reached a stage in which the movement of people, in the older sense, is no longer necessary. The universal diffusion of the art of printing has so made the world one, that an advance in medicine rising in any part of the earth rapidly becomes the property of the whole. Even in the later phases of the history of medicine, however, the course has not been wholly one of progress. The history of the practice of blood-letting, which this country acquired in the schools of Italy and Spain as a legacy from the medicine of Greece and Arabia, cannot be regarded as an example of progress. At the present time I believe that we are witnessing a similar exaggerated and uncritical application of the introduced art of massage. Nevertheless, behind all these exaggerations and misapplications of introduced practices, which still occur in the practice of medicine, and behind all the transformations which have characterized the different stages of its history, there stands out the vast importance of the contact of peoples and the blending of their cultures as a main, if not the chief, source of progress. The earlier history of mankind seems to have been one in which different parts of the earth were subject to long periods of isolation, relative or complete, in which progress stagnated or turned to degeneration. Then came some movement of mankind by which elements of culture were diffused and, when transplanted into places where culture had stagnated, acted as the stimuli to new processes of evolution and progress. The nature of the process which took place in each region depended on many things: on the nature of the indigenous culture and of the new elements; on the relative numbers of the migrant and indigenous peoples; on the difference in the level of their cultures; on the nature of the interaction between the two peoples, whether peaceful or warlike; and on many other factors.

THE EFFECT ON MEDICINE OF MIXTURE OF CULTURES

Of especial importance, so far as medicine is concerned, has been the prevailing tendency of the indigenous culture in the direction of magic or religion. When a people stand at a level of culture in which medicine has a rational basis, so that its practice rests on principles deserving to be ranked as scientific, the mixture of cultures will lead to development in medicine. Introduced medical practices will not only stimulate the growth of the indigenous art, but may lead to modification of the introduced practice, modifications designed to make it a more fit instrument with which to combat disease. If, on the other hand, the indigenous culture is dominated wholly by the religious attitude, the result, unless the introducers of the new art are especially numerous or powerful, may only be to deprive this of the purpose to which it is primarily adapted, and to convert it into a practice so closely associated with religion, and apparently partaking so wholly of the religious spirit that it may be difficult to recognize in it any relation to the art of medicine.

Similarly, if the indigenous people are wholly given over to magic, an introduced medical practice may so assimilate itself with the native mode of thought that again its medical character and rational basis may be lost or greatly obscured.

Not only does the comparative study of medicine, magic, and religion serve well to illustrate the complex character of human progress, but it may also teach us much concerning the nature of the evolutionary process by which the complexity is brought about. It is generally held that one of the chief features of the process of evolution is the increase in specialization of function. That the evolution of human society is generally characterized by such increasing specialization of social function stands beyond all doubt. We can have no better example of it than the differentiation between the leech, sorcerer, and priest, which has occurred in the history of medicine, magic, and religion. It is a question, however, whether increasing specialization is characteristic of evolution throughout, or whether it is not rather a necessary feature. I should like to call it even a necessary evil feature of the middle stages of evolution. I believe that there are now becoming apparent, in many departments of social life (I recognize it especially in that of science), indications that specialization can be carried too far, and that with further advance we may come again to those close interrelations between the different aspects of human culture which are characteristic of its earlier stages.

THE RELATIONS BETWEEN MEDICINE AND RELIGION

I will conclude by considering briefly whether this movement contrary to, or across, the growth of specialization is not illustrated by the relations between medicine and religion.

In the first part of the book I considered briefly the part taken by faith and suggestion in the success of the measures by which the ruder forms of human society have endeavoured to overcome the effects of disease. It is the firm belief of savage and barbarous peoples in the efficacy of the rites carried out by the leech, sorcerer, and priest which is the most frequent cause of their success. As medicine has progressed and has been differentiated from magic and religion, this play of psychical factors has not ceased. Few can now be found who will deny that the success which attended the complex prescriptions, and most of the dietetic remedies of the last generation, was due mainly, if not entirely, to the play of faith and suggestion. The salient feature of the medicine of to-day is that these psychical factors are no longer allowed to play their part unwittingly, but are themselves becoming the subject of study, so that the present age is seeing the growth of a rational system of psycho-therapeutics. One feature of this system, which is already becoming clear, is that it must take account of agencies which have till now been held to be the function of the priest rather than of the physician. If medicine is to maintain its hold on certain aspects of disease which should come properly within its sphere, it must find that it has much to learn from the priest, if, indeed, some kind of collaboration between the two is not often desirable. A striking feature of the last twenty years in this country is the frequent combination of priest and physician in one person, while in America, a regular system of collaboration between the two has come into being in what is known as the Emmanuel movement.[1]

As medicine comes to extend its scope to the wider study of disorder of the mind, and reaches a higher recognition of the part taken by psychical factors in the causation and treatment of disease, not only will the work of the physician be found to overlap the function of the priest, but also those of the teacher, the jurist, the moralist, the social reformer. Just as there are problems and individual cases of disease which need the collaboration of priest and physician, so are there cases in which the physician, the teacher, the moral and social reformer, can help one another far more profoundly and successfully than they have done in the past.

The study of the latest phase of the history of medicine shows us a limit to the increasing specialization of function as a character of social evolution. The relations which seem to be coming into existence between medicine and religion resemble in some degree those which we have seen to characterize the early phases of its history. They differ chiefly in that the later phase recognizes explicitly, and is learning to understand, a set of conditions which were once allowed to play their part unregarded and

[1] See *Religion and Medicine*, by E. Worcester, S. McComb, and I. H. Coriat, London, 1908.

unstudied. In the domain of the medicine of the mind—and its scope is far wider than is usually supposed—the course of history seems to be showing us that the close interdependence of different departments of human culture will be just as much a character of its latest and its highest phase, as it was characteristic of its earliest and its lowest.

5

MIND AND MEDICINE[1]

The early relationships between mind and medicine are ultimately bound up with the process by which medicine grew out of magic and religion. The history of medicine reveals a long and chequered progress, still far from complete, in which Man's attitude towards disease slowly became different from that he held towards the many other mysteries by which he was surrounded. His endeavours to cope with disease took at first two directions. In one he ascribed disease to the action of beings different from himself, but capable of being reached by rites of prayer and propitiation. Since these rites, wherever we study them, reveal an attitude of respect and appeal and imply powers which man does not himself possess, it seems legitimate to regard the beings to whom they are addressed as higher and more powerful than himself. The general body of rites and beliefs forming the means of intercourse between Man and these

[1] [A Lecture delivered in the John Rylands Library, the 9th of April, 1919. For permission to reprint this lecture I am indebted to the Chief Librarian, Dr. Henry Guppy.]

higher powers make up the aspect of life we call religion. One of Man's early modes of behaviour towards disease may thus be regarded as forming part of religion and the religious attitude.

In the other direction disease was ascribed to the action of other human beings, or of beings of a non-human kind believed to be amenable to processes of a compulsive nature, and therefore less powerful than Man himself, so that the attitude adopted towards them implied neither respect nor appeal. When his efforts to deal with disease took this direction, Man compelled or induced the being to whom disease was ascribed to withdraw the agencies by which the illness was being produced, or himself employed measures designed to negative their effects. Beliefs and measures of this kind make up the aspect of life known as magic, but this aspect is less capable of definition than religion and needs analysis into several distinct elements. One of these is certainly degenerate religion, beliefs and rites no longer implying any reference to higher powers which at one time formed their motive and sanction.

The great majority of the measures by which existing savage peoples attempt to cope with disease fall into one or other of the two categories of religion and magic. All that we know of the history of mankind suggests that it was only after long ages, and in some few parts of the earth, that Man reached a conception of disease according to which it is ascribed to processes similar to those underlying modern systems of medicine. The emergence of medicine from its intimate associations with religion and magic is closely connected with the gradual substitution of the concept of physical causation for the spiritualistic agencies of the animism which formed the early attitude towards nature. The growth of medicine is closely bound up with the development of the concept of a natural world as opposed to a world we now regard as supernatural.

All the evidence at our command goes to show that, as Man relinquished his early animistic interpretation of the universe, this was replaced by explanations of a materialistic kind. In so far as events were not ascribed to spiritual beings or to direct human agency, they were believed to depend on the action of material agents. The agents thus supposed to be effective in the production of disease during the history of medicine have been of two chief kinds. Among peoples who have been especially influenced by beliefs concerning animals, this branch of creation has been prominent in their theories concerning the production of disease. Elsewhere the evident connexion of the blood with life has led to the belief that disease is predominantly due to an altered character of this fluid, and this belief formed the starting-point of the humoral pathology which for so many centuries formed the basis of medicine. The two great developments of our own time in medicine have followed these two main lines of early belief. For the worms and snakes[1] of savage medicine have been substituted the microscopic and ultra-microscopic organisms of the germ theory of disease, while the place of the old humours has been taken by the alteration in the proper proportion of internal secretions which is now coming to be recognized as the immediate cause of so many morbid states.

During the long period in which medicine was occupied in substituting these material agents for the spiritual beings to which all disease was once ascribed, little if any room was left for agencies which come within the modern connotation of mind.

When Man thought of the production of disease by other than material agents, his concept of the activity involved was very different from that of "mind" as held by ourselves, or at any rate by the psychologist. The agency to which he ascribed disease was spiritual rather than mental, and was conceived as having

---

[1] When these early beliefs are regarded as previsions of the germ-theory, it should be remembered how naturally they follow from the general beliefs concerning animals characteristic of certain forms of human culture.

form and capacity for independent existence. It might be a spirit which had never been human or had human associations, or one which had once had a human habitation, but had come through the death of its host to acquire an independent existence, or, lastly, it might be a soul which still had its customary seat within a human body, but could leave it in sleep or trance to act as the producer of disease.

Though at this stage of human culture there is no trace of the modern concept of mind as distinguished from spirit, we can see clearly that most of the processes by which disease was thought to be produced and was treated are such as would act through the mind. The manifold lines of treatment by which human or spiritual agents were induced to cure disease acted, if they were successful, through the agency of faith and suggestion. The curative measures, which are still being employed by many peoples, act through the same processes, and owe their success to the faith they inspire, or to the more mysterious property we call suggestion.

It is necessary, however, to distinguish the production and treatment of disease by agencies acting through the mind from the knowledge that the measures used act in this manner. Though remedies acting through the mind were probably the earliest to be employed by Man, the knowledge that the remedies act in this way is one of the most recent acquirements of medicine. It is said that the Japanese of the sixteenth century understood the action of remedies through the mind,[1] while the great importance attached by the Hindus to the mental, as opposed to the material, makes it probable that they also had more than an inkling of the rôle of mental factors in the treatment, if not in the production, of disease. How far this may be so must be left to special students who will examine the original authorities with an eye to the possibility that the agencies in

[1] M. Neuburger, *History of Medicine*, London, 1910, vol. i, p. 78.

which these peoples believed were spiritual rather than mental in nature. If we confine our attention to our own culture, it is only within the last fifty or sixty years that there has been any clear recognition of the vast importance of the mental factor in the production and treatment of disease, and even now this knowledge is far from being fully recognized either by the medical profession or the laity.

For the first definite movement in this direction we have, as so often happens in the history of human culture, to thank external influence, in this case that of India. The first great stimulus to the study of the mental factor in disease came from the need to understand the mysterious action of hypnotism. Though this agency had long been known in Europe, as in all other parts of the world, and had been brought prominently to notice at the end of the eighteenth century by the activity of Mesmer, the knowledge which the Abbé Faria brought to Europe from India acted as a great stimulus to its scientific study, in which Braid of Manchester holds a foremost place, while the later experience of Esdaile in India did much to help the practical utilization of hypnotism in this country.

About this time there was setting in the wave of materialism which was to dominate European thought for many years. Under this influence the new agent was regarded as a form of magnetism or other physical force. It was only slowly that there came into being the now generally accepted view that the agency through which hypnotism produces its effects is suggestion. This is a process comparable with volition, imagination, or other similar concepts which, wholly devoid of any implication of the independent action of a spiritual being, had been reached by the new and slowly developing science of psychology. The study of hypnotism and allied processes led students to distinguish clearly the important influence of suggestion in the production and treatment of disease.

The phenomena of hypnotism having led students to the

definite recognition of the mental factor in medicine, it was natural that attention should be directed to the influence of other mental conditions. This development followed many directions. The general public, less under the influence of the prevailing materialism of science than the medical profession, and more ready to accept any new doctrine which could be made to harmonize with the old spiritualistic view of disease, adopted with enthusiasm many new systems of healing. In most of these the vast power of religious faith was explicitly recognized. In some, such as Christian Science and the "New Thought", etc., the cardinal element of faith was made the starting-point of intellectual constructions, which gave, or seemed to the believers to give, a rational basis for the success that these new movements so often obtained. At the same time, within the medical profession, especially among French-speaking peoples, there came into existence a definite system of psycho-therapeutics in which suggestion and other agencies were assigned their rôles, and principles were laid down to indicate the scope of these agencies and the means of turning them to best advantage. In Switzerland P. Dubois[1] laid stress on the helpfulness of explaining what he called the philosophy of disease, while in France J. Déjérine and E. Gauckler,[2] in more scientific fashion, compiled a most valuable textbook of the principles and methods of psycho-therapy.

Independently, growing out of dissatisfaction with the practical use of hypnotism, a third line of approach was taken by the Viennese physician, Sigmund Freud. It had been found by earlier workers that hypnotism was often the means of reaching experience which had been so completely forgotten that by no effort

[1] *Les Psychonéuroses et leur traitement moral*, Paris, 1908; translated by S. E. Jelliffe and W. A. White as *The Psychic Treatment of Nervous Diseases*, New York and London, 1906.

[2] *Les Manifestations fonctionelles des psychonéuroses*, Paris, 1911; translated by S. E. Jelliffe as *The Psychoneuroses and their Treatment by Psychotherapy*, Philadelphia and London, 1913.

of the will could it be recalled. Working in conjunction with Breuer,[1] Freud found the process of bringing these buried memories to the surface led to the disappearance of hysterical symptoms of long duration, and the two authors founded upon this experience a theory of hysteria according to which its symptoms are the indirect expression of old mental injuries (traumata), especially those of early childhood.

Later, Freud found that the buried memories which manifested themselves in this morbid manner could be brought to the surface more securely and with greater therapeutic efficacy, though less expeditiously, without the aid of hypnotism. By means of his method of free association, starting as a rule from clues provided by dreams, Freud was led to formulate a theory of the unconscious and an elaborate scheme of the mechanism by which it is related to and acts upon the conscious. In the course of this work Freud was led to the conclusion that the mental experience which had been cut off from the general body of consciousness was nearly always connected with sex. His work, and still more that of his disciples, came to deal so exclusively with sexual factors that the general body both of the medical profession and the laity refused to give this movement the attention it deserved. They failed to recognize the immense importance of the mental mechanisms laid bare by Freud's method of analysis, and the body of evidence which was thereby provided to illustrate the influence of the unconscious.

One of the most important aspects of Freud's work was that the rôle he assigned to the unconscious enabled him to adopt in the most complete manner the principle of determinism within the mental sphere which had been of such value in the progress of physical science. It is essential to this progress that the student shall believe implicitly, or at the least act as if he so

[1] S. Freud, *Selected Papers of Hysteria and other Psychoneuroses* (Nervous and Mental Disease Monograph Series, No. 4), New York, 1912.

believe, that every physical event has its physical antecedent, without the presence of which it would not itself have come into existence. The progress of physical science depends largely on the robustness of the faith in this law of causation, which allows no residue or anomaly, however insignificant it may seem, to be put on one side as due to chance or accident. The successful worker in science makes such residue or anomaly the subject of patient investigation until its occurrence has been traced to its antecedents, antecedents which may open new paths to the understanding of experience which till then had had no adequate explanation.

So long as the attention of students of mind was confined to the sphere of the definitely conscious, there was no opening for the application of a similar doctrine of determinism within the sphere of the mental. Recognizing that the principle of psychical determinism must hold good if psychology is to become a science, some students had put forward hypothetical mental dispositions where no antecedents could be detected in consciousness, but these were too vague to be of any assistance in research. It is of no service to postulate a disposition of which one knows nothing, which stands in no known relation to any other part of construction. Other students definitely threw over any attempt to apply the principle of determinism within the sphere of mind, and were content to seek for physical causes in the form of physiological processes or dispositions whenever the study of conscious process failed to provide an adequate explanation.

The special value of Freud's work is due to the fact that he was not content merely to put forward unconscious dispositions as the antecedents of changes in consciousness, but was enabled by the knowledge derived from his analyses to formulate a definite scheme of the unconscious region of the mind and of its relation to the conscious. This scheme is of necessity to a large extent hypothetical, and as with all hypotheses of such complexity, it will certainly require modification, but growing experience is pointing more and more surely to the truth of its main assumptions.

For several years before the outbreak of the war many were coming to acknowledge the great importance of mental factors in the production and cure not only of diseases obviously mental in nature, but also of many which had been held to be wholly physical. There was, however, no general agreement concerning the principles which should underlie a system of psychological medicine. There was even no general belief in the possibility of principles which could act as the basis and inspiration of research. From the one system which could have provided such basis and inspiration the majority of workers were estranged, partly owing to the undue weight laid upon sex by its adherents, partly owing to the unsatisfactory form in which the new doctrines had been put before the public.

The effect of their recent experience upon the opinions of the medical profession has been profound. Perhaps the most striking feature of the war from the medical point of view has been the enormous scale upon which its conditions have produced functional nervous disorders, a scale far surpassing any previous war, although the Russo-Japanese campaign gave indications of the mental and nervous havoc which the conditions of modern warfare are able to produce. While certain of these disorders are the result in part of physical causes, such as cerebral concussion or illnesses specially affecting the nervous system, it has gradually become clear, even to the firmest believer in the dependence of mind on body, that in the great majority of cases the conditions upon which the disorder depends are purely mental. All are coming to see the profound effect of mental shock and strain in weakening the powers of control by which instinctive processes are normally held in check, if not completely suppressed. Moreover, it has become clear that, in the vast majority of cases, the morbid processes which have been set up by shock or strain are not connected with the sexual instinct, but depend on the awakening of suppressed tendencies connected with the still more fundamental instinct of self-preservation. While the nature of the war-neuroses is satisfactorily explained by the Freudian mechanisms of suppression, conversion, defence-reaction, compromise-formation, etc., they lend no support to the exclusively sexual origin of neurosis, which has been the chief obstacle to the general acceptance of Freud's doctrines. It cannot yet be said that the essential features of these doctrines have met with general acceptance, but the state of the matter is now very different from the widespread neglect, or even reprobation, which existed before the war. The great majority of students of the neuroses are now prepared to consider Freud's position, to accept such parts of his doctrine as seem to them supported by the facts, and to suspend judgment concerning those parts for the truth of which they do not deem the existing evidence sufficient.

I have dealt at length with the controversial topic of Freud's views concerning the neuroses because he, more than any other worker, has emphasized the mental factor in disease and more thoroughly than any one else has based his work on a determinism which is as essential to the progress of psychology and psycho-pathology as determinism within the physical sphere is essential to the progress of the sciences which deal with the material world.

In the foregoing sketch of the history of the relations between mind and medicine I have considered at some length one of the most important principles of psychological medicine, viz. the principle of psychical determinism. This principle is of especial importance in connexion with the art of diagnosis, for only those who believe firmly that every mental symptom has its mental antecedent will have the patience and courage to probe deeply enough into the history of a patient. They will not rest content until they have discovered not only the events which acted as the immediate conditions of the disease, but also those factors producing the special qualities of the patient's mental constitution which made it possible for these conditions to produce so great and so disastrous an effect. A firm belief in the principle of psychical determinism is the most important condition of success in the diagnosis and treatment of functional nervous disorders.

I propose now to consider some other of the more important principles which underlie success in the treatment of these disorders. One such principle may be regarded as a consequence of psychical determinism. It is a general rule of medicine that the physician must not be content to treat symptoms, but having traced these symptoms to their source, should by suitable remedies attack this source and treat the symptoms through the conditions by which they have been produced. This principle holds good for psychological medicine. If it is believed that the symptoms have been produced by psychical factors, it will follow that the remedies must also be psychical in nature. I do not suppose that even the crudest materialist, having once acknowledged that the symptoms depend upon a fright in childhood, a reproach concerning a misdemeanour in youth, or an anxiety in adult life, would expect to produce any permanent improvement by the administration of a drug or the performance of a surgical operation. It must be pointed out, however, that such measures may be successful in some cases, not merely through their psychical effort, but because, by removing secondary disturbances, they may break a vicious circle and thereby give an opening for the action of intrinsic mental forces working towards recovery. The vis medicatrix naturæ applies in the mental as well as in the material sphere.

Another principle which is now meeting with general acceptance in psychological medicine is that functional nervous and mental disorders depend essentially on disturbance of the instinctive and emotional or affective aspects of the mind. It is now widely acknowledged that in the attempt to get back to the roots of these disorders it is necessary to look for experience which had a strong emotional tone. This principle has long been more or less explicitly recognized and underlies such general beliefs as are expressed in the adage that it is worry and not work which kills. But it is only recently that we have learnt to appreciate the extent of its application and to use it in treatment as a guide of the first importance. It has long been known that, in the more explicitly mental disorders of insanity, no good is done by reasoning with the patient as a means of countering his delusions. It seems even that such reasoning may only intensify and fix the delusions by driving the patient to adopt the part of an advocate. We now see that this is a necessary consequence of the emotional basis of the disorder. The delusions are the product of a process of rationalization, by means of which the patient has tried to account for his abnormal emotional state. Treatment directed to these secondary products wholly fails to touch the deeper and essential factors.

The modern theory of emotion connects it closely with instinct. There is reason to believe that the emotional factor in neurosis is the expression of some instinctive tendency which has been suppressed on account of its incompatibility with social standards. Neurosis occurs when, through some shock or strain, the agencies which keep the tendency in check are weakened, allowing it again to come in to conflict with social standards. The form which the neurosis takes depends on the process by which Nature attempts to solve this conflict.[1]

I must be content with this brief description of some of the more important principles upon which rests our modern system of psycho-therapy, and pass on to consider some of the main agencies which are utilized by the practitioners of this branch of

---

[1] See *British Journ. Psych.*, 1918, vol. ix, p. 236, and *Mental Hygiene*, 1918, vol. ii, p. 513.

medicine. I shall lay stress especially on the three agencies of self-knowledge, self-reliance, and suggestion.

The agency of self-knowledge, which, following Dr. W. Brown, I have elsewhere[1] called autognosis, covers a wide field in which two main sections can be distinguished. Where the morbid state depends on some experience or tendency which lies within the region of the unconscious, self-knowledge as a therapeutic agency will consist in bringing the buried and unconscious experience to the surface. The unconscious experience has to be brought into relation with the general body of experience, which is readily accessible to consciousness, and so made part of it that it ceases to act as a separate force in conflict with the general body of conscious experience.

The other main form of the agency of self-knowledge comprises the processes by which a sufferer is brought to understand elements of conscious experience which are being misinterpreted, and through this misunderstanding are helping to maintain, even if they did not help to produce, the morbid state.

Between these two forms lie a large variety of processes in which there is a mingling of the unconscious and conscious elements brought into relation with one another, thus doing away with the conflicts upon which the disorder depends and restoring harmony within the personality.

It may seem that the rôle here assigned to the process of self-knowledge is in contradiction with what has been said earlier concerning the failure of appeal to the intellectual, and the necessity of attacking the instinctive and emotional basis of the disorder. The intellectual element, however, though secondary, is present and must not be neglected. Experience shows that, while the direct attack upon the intellectual aspect of a neurosis or

---

[1] Art. "Psycho-therapeutics", Hastings' *Encyclopædia of Comparative Religion and Ethics*, vol. x, p. 433. This article may be consulted for information concerning other therapeutic agencies which I do not consider in this chapter.

psychosis will fail, a line of treatment in which the intelligence of the patient is brought to bear on the part taken by instinctive and emotional factors in the production of his illness may be of the utmost value. Indeed, success in treatment depends largely on the possibility of diverting the intellectual activity from a channel which is forcing it into an asocial or antisocial direction, and leading it into one which will again enable the patient to live in harmony with the society to which he belongs.

Where the sufferer from neurosis is intelligent, the mere exposure of the faulty trend, and the demonstration of the process in which this trend took its origin, may be sufficient. The patient only needs to be started on the right path, and his own intelligence will lead him back to health and happiness. In other cases the faulty trend has been so long in action that a lengthy process of re-education may be necessary to put the morbid process in the proper light, and reduce the power which through habit has been acquired by the secondary products of the morbid process. In other cases, again, the intelligence of the patient may not be sufficient to enable him to solve the conflict unaided, and the process of re-education has to assist the patient to understand the nature of his disorder and the processes by which he can again place his steps upon the path of health.

The next agency I have to consider is one which may be summed up under the term self-reliance. There is a pronounced tendency for sufferers from neurosis to avoid the unpleasant at all costs. Since all social duties, even those in which the nearest relatives are involved, are liable to become irksome or positively distressing, the patient seeks quiet and solitude, and if left alone these antisocial tendencies may become a habit, converting one who before his illness was a social favourite into a recluse or misanthrope. Aches and bodily discomforts which in health are disregarded, and when so treated soon cease to annoy, are liable in neurosis to grow in intensity and insistence. They may so absorb the attention that the sufferer's efforts are exclusively devoted to the avoidance of all conditions, such as noise and excitement, which aggravate, or seem to him to aggravate, his troubles. He is apt to resort to drugs, either at his own or his physician's instance, and since these are merely palliative and do not touch the roots of his malady, they only serve to accentuate his pains and worries, even if he escapes the greater evil of a definite drug-habit. He strives to banish from his mind all distressing thoughts and memories, including experience so arresting that, if his efforts were not exclusively turned towards the avoidance of immediate pain, he would at once recognize the futility of his attempt.

One of the first steps in the treatment of such cases is to persuade the patient to forego any adventitious aids, such as drugs or electricity, upon which he has come to rely. Assisted by a process of re-education designed to show their subjective nature, he must be encouraged to fight his pains and discomforts by his own strength. He must be convinced of the futility of his attempts to escape from the thoughts and memories which distress him, and shown by trial that when these painful experiences are faced they are far less terrible than they seem to be when kept at a distance. He must be encouraged to mix with his fellows in spite of the immediate discomfort which this produces, and here again he must learn by experience that the pains of the reality do not equal those of anticipation.

The policy of facing his troubles instead of running away from them has certain effects of a far-reaching kind, which are due to a special mode of reaction of the mind when in the presence of the painful. By repressing unpleasant thoughts and memories the patient is assisting a process by which we tend to suppress painful experience and dissociate it from the general body of consciousness. When thus suppressed and dissociated, however, such experience does not cease to exist, but by its activity produces many of the most painful features of the illness, distressing dreams and nightmares being the symptoms which form the most direct consequence of the repression and suppression. By facing his troubles in place of striving to banish them, the dreams or other troubles due to repression may disappear, or so alter their character as not to interfere with comfort and health.[1] Owing to the malign power of repressed experience, the policy of facing the painful may have effects reaching far more widely than might be expected from the normal experience of health, that a trouble faced loses half its terror.

The third agency I have to consider is suggestion. Though this term is freely and confidently used in psychological medicine, there is little agreement concerning its exact meaning, and much is included among its activities which has little to do with it in nature.[2] I use the term for a process which belongs essentially to the instinctive side of mind. It is the representative in Man of one aspect of the gregarious instinct, the instinct which makes it possible for all the members of a group to act in unison so that they seem to be actuated by a common purpose. According to this view it is a process which differs essentially in nature from those mental processes which produce uniformity of behaviour by endowing the members of a group with a common idea or a common sentiment. Its activities lie definitely within the unconscious sphere, so that when the physician employs suggestion consciously he is using in an artificial manner an agency which belongs properly to the region of the unconscious.

The most striking form in which Man has come to use suggestion consciously and wittingly is hypnotism. All gradations are met in practice between this definitely conscious use, and cases in which the physician acts upon his patient and moulds him to

---

[1] For examples of the beneficial effects of this kind see *The Repression of War Experience*, Proc. Roy. Soc. of Med., 1918 (Section of Psychiatry), vol. xi, p. 1.

[2] For its distinction from faith as a therapeutic agency, see Art. "Psychotherapeutics" in Hastings' *Encyclopædia*.

his will by the unconscious process of suggestion, without recognizing the true nature of the process which is taking place. As a rule, the more unwitting the use of suggestion the greater is its power and efficacy. On this foundation rests the success of quacks, for they advocate and use their nostrums in blissful ignorance of the process upon which their efficacy really depends. The physician who knows enough to distinguish between the influence of suggestion and other modes of action a remedy possesses, may signally fail to attain the success of a quack because the instinctive process of suggestion is not being employed in the manner natural to it.

One of the greatest difficulties of psychological medicine arises out of the opposition, if it be not definite incompatibility, between suggestion and the group of agencies which rest upon the principle of self-reliance. The action of suggestion can never be excluded in any form of medical treatment, whether it be explicitly designed to act upon the mind or whether ostensibly it is purely physical in character. It is when suggestion is used wittingly, and especially when it is directed to produce a definite hypnotic or hypnoidal state, that the conflict with the principle of self-reliance becomes most definite. In these cases the patient is definitely led to rely on a power, in this case that of the phys- ician, other than his own. Even when, as in the most recent developments of hypnotic treatment, suggestions are given in the hypnotic state designed to strengthen the self-reliance and volitional control of the patient, he cannot have the confidence, and especially the confidence in the future, which is given by a recovery which he can clearly trace to his own efforts. The whole process differs essentially from that in which the action of the physician has been limited to helping the agency of self- knowledge and placing the steps of the patient on the right path. Even if the hypnotic suggestion should succeed in strengthening the will and assisting the patient to face his troubles, his satisfac- tion and confidence must in some degree be tarnished by the knowledge that this result is due to the action of another person and not to his own activity.

There is also a certain amount of conflict between hypnotic treatment and remedies which rest on the principle of self-knowledge. We do not yet understand the nature of hypnotism. Even to the physician this remedy partakes of that mysterious character which belongs to aspects of nature which have not yet been brought into relation with the rest of our scientific knowledge. To the patient, this mystic character must be far greater. In a fully satisfactory system of mental medicine the treatment should follow logically from the pathology. The remedies should stand in a definite and intelligible relation to the causes by which the illness has been produced, and the processes by which these causes have produced their effects. The intrusion of a mysterious agency interrupts the continuity of blended diagnosis and treatment. It disturbs the process by which the patient is led towards recovery by knowledge of the conditions through which he was led astray.

In spite of these difficulties arising out of conflicts with the main principles of psycho-therapy, there are certain cases in which the use of hypnotism is justified. A faulty trend of thought or conduct may by habit have become so fixed that it requires a process more drastic than mere persuasion to break it, or the unaided strength of the patient may be insufficient to enable him to stand up against the pains or horrors of his malady. In such cases the experience which has produced or helped to produce his illness may by this treatment be buried still more deeply than before; no lasting and complete success can be expected unless the treatment is continued sooner or later in accordance with the leading principles of self-knowledge and self-reliance. If, however, the patient can be protected from undue stress, hypnotic or other form of suggestive treatment may enable him to pass through life without manifest nervous or mental disorder.

Another and perhaps more legitimate mode of using hypnosis

is in the interest of diagnosis. Dissociated or forgotten experience may be recovered more speedily by means of hypnosis than by the process of free association, the analysis of dreams, or other means of gaining access to the unconscious. Such use of hypnotism as an instrument of self-knowledge need interfere very little with the principle of self-reliance, the hypnotic process merely giving the knowledge from which the therapeutic process starts and upon which it is based.

Though hypnotic treatment can thus be justified in certain cases, it is rarely necessary. It is generally used, firstly as a short cut to immediate results without regard to the future, and secondly, because the striking and theatrical character of these results greatly impresses a public accustomed to consider the needs of the moment as more important than a complete and lasting cure.

I must be content with this brief account of a few of the more important principles of mental therapy and of the agencies which are available in putting these principles into practice. I shall conclude this chapter by pointing out that these basic principles of mental medicine are also those of all sound systems of education, and underlie success in social life, in health, as well as in disease.

In the case of one process, the attainment of self-knowledge as a means of treatment, the resemblance with a social process of normal health is so obvious that the physician has come to use a term derived therefrom. The process by which a faulty trend of feeling, thought, or conduct is diverted into a more healthy channel is generally known as re-education. This only differs from the ordinary process of education in the nature of the knowledge and attitude to be acquired. The agency of self-reliance, which I have made of such fundamental importance in psycho-therapy, is of equally great importance in education, though this importance is inadequately recognized in modern educational practice. This failure is due to the fact that it is far easier to pour facts into a pupil than to develop an attitude of mind, just as it is far easier to pour medicine into a patient than to instil hope, patience, and self-reliance.

The influence of suggestion in education resembles in many respects that which I have assigned to it in medicine, and is of especial importance owing to the great suggestibility of children. The importance lies in the power of suggestion in relation to that function of education by which it develops an attitude of interest in the intellectual, the beautiful, or the noble. Nothing assists the development of such an attitude more than the mental atmosphere which the teacher has produced, just as no factor is of greater importance in therapeutics than the atmosphere of hope and trust produced, whether in home or hospital, by a skilful physician. In each case this atmosphere is produced in the main by suggestion, and in education as in medicine this success is the greater the more unwittingly this agency is used. The success of a great teacher, or that which so often comes to new movements in education, even when based on wrong principles, is due to the infective enthusiasm and personality of the teacher acting through an agency quite distinct from the matter he teaches. As in medicine, the danger to which such a teacher is open is that he may rely too greatly on this influence, and fail to recognize its conflict with the principles of self-knowledge and self-reliance.

The principles which I have here put forward as suited for the treatment of mental disorders of the individual are equally appropriate to the treatment of the faulty trends and disorders of society as a whole. The statesman whose duty it is to find remedies for such faulty trends and disorders has, like the physician of the individual, to discover the deeper conditions by which they have been produced, and may do much to amend the evil by remedies based upon this knowledge. He can hardly, however, expect a lasting cure unless he tell the people what is wrong and where they have gone astray. Without such self-knowledge his work is liable to be upset by later conditions which would be innocuous if the community had been led to see and understand the nature of their earlier misfortunes.

Moreover, the self-knowledge of the community is like that of the individual in that the social group is even more subject than the individuals of which it is composed to the influence of conditions lying deeply beneath the surface. It is generally recognized that the factors upon which social disorders depend usually go far back in the history of the people, factors, not only in conflict with later social standards, but also in many cases with existing social conditions. To understand the evil and find the right remedy, inquiries are needed which go so far into the past that they lie altogether outside the memories of the people and can only be reached by special processes of historical research and sociological reasoning. These factors belong just as much to the unconscious of the folk-mind as the factors producing a neurosis or psychosis belong to the unconscious region of the individual mind.

The importance of self-reliance in disorders of the body politic is as great as that of self-knowledge. A nation which refuses to face the facts and is content to swallow every placebo and nostrum of its politicians cannot expect to gain thereby the permanent improvement of any disorders by which it is effected. Even if the remedies of its rulers be wise, only a temporary effect can be expected if the people rely too much on this wisdom, and fail to make a united effort to remedy the faults of their society.

It is less easy to compare the rôle of suggestion in the group with that it takes in determining the fate of the individual. Suggestion is essentially a process tending to produce unanimity in the social group, and its action is even more inevitable when we are dealing with social than with individual disorders. The physician who knows that suggestion cannot be excluded, but that its influence may be for good or evil, will be forewarned and forearmed, and this is equally true of the statesman. Suggestion is responsible for panic or collapse, just as it may be responsible for harmony to a more useful end. The wise statesman who understands the pervasive and yet elusive nature of this agency may by such understanding do much to avert its more malign aspects and turn it to a useful purpose, while a people who understand may be prevented from falling victims to the excesses of which this agency is capable. In the society, as with the individual, the potency of suggestion is the greater, the more unwittingly it is in action. And as in medicine its greatest dangers may be averted through knowledge, so may much be done to avert danger and make suggestion an instrument for good in social and political life if its nature and mode of action are understood.

Closely connected both with education and statesmanship is the subject of ethical training. Here the importance of self-knowledge and self-reliance is so well recognized that it is not necessary to dwell upon it at length. It must be enough to point out that the principles so universally accepted as the means of treating faulty trends in those aspects of behaviour which, though clearly abnormal, are yet usually regarded as lying within the bounds of health, have been shown in this lecture to hold good for the correction of morbid tendencies which lie definitely within the region of disease. The modern theory of psychological medicine supports the close relation between mental disease and crime to which all recent developments in sociology and jurisprudence are tending. Moreover, if the principles of psychological medicine here put forward are accepted, they should remove, or go far towards removing, the obstacle to the acceptance of this close relation which is presented by the problem of moral responsibility. It will be seen that the recognition of crime as a manifestation of disease, far from implying an absence of responsibility, would on the lines laid down in this lecture lead us logically to treatment which does not differ greatly from that implying such responsibility. The mode of treating crime and moral disorder which is suggested by its relationship to disease differs from the older method, in that the erring person would not be merely exhorted to exert his will, but would be shown how his faulty trend has been produced, and would thus be assisted in the application of his voluntary efforts.

It is a striking fact that the organization which has by long experience acquired the most highly developed system of treating moral defect, the Catholic Church, lays great stress on the apparently minor faults which have led up to definitely immoral conduct, and directs the attention and efforts of the penitent to these quite as much as to the conduct which is the immediate occasion for penance. This close resemblance of the traditional practice of the Catholic Church with that of the most modern systems of psycho-therapy leads me to the place of religion in psychological medicine. From one point of view the use of religious motives in treating mental disorder is definitely in conflict with the principle of self-reliance. For the essence of religion is that it inculcates reliance upon a power other than that of the sufferer. Some degree of such conflict there must always be, and in many of the forms in which religion is adopted as a therapeutic agency this conflict is pronounced. But in the most recent developments of religious doctrine, in which it is recognized that the higher power acts through normal mental process, the conflict becomes of no great account. The modern religious teacher does not tell the sufferer that he will get rid of his troubles by the mere act of faith, but counsels self-examination and self-help. To put his advice into simple language, he says that God only helps those who help themselves, and thus adopts a line which in essentials is that advocated in this lecture. In thus treating religion as a therapeutic agency, I recognize that I am dealing only with one aspect of the matter. I could not, however, leave the subject wholly on one side. It is necessary that those who employ religious agencies in the treatment of disease, whether they be physicians or priests, should realize that in so doing they are running in some degree counter to one of the principles of psychological medicine, for if this fact is recognized they will avoid the evils which might accompany too crude an application of the religious agency. Moreover, no treatment of the subject of mind and medicine would be complete which ignores religion. One of the most striking results of the modern developments of our knowledge concerning the influence of mental factors in disease is that they are bringing back medicine in some measure to that co-operation with religion which existed in the early stages of human progress.

INDEX